The Fledglings Way to Mediumship

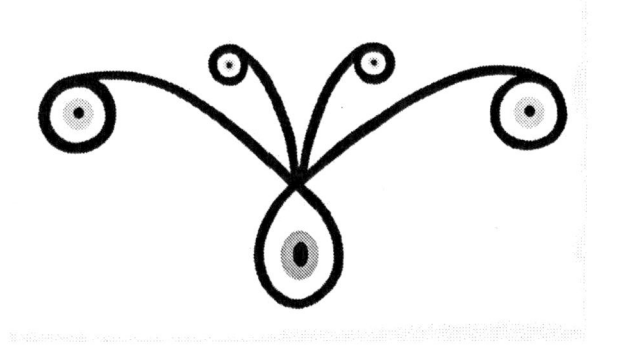

First Published in 2003

The Fledglings Way to Mediumship

How to become a good and honest Psychic Medium

Our Life is an Open Book   But We Write the Pages!

Agnes Freeman

This is a book of learning for all who are interested in Psychic Development

Copyright © 2003 Agnes Freeman

Apart from any fair dealing for the purposes of research or private study, or criticism or review, as permitted under the Copyright, Designs and Patents Act 1988, this publication may only be reproduced, stored or transmitted, in any form or by any means, with the prior permission in writing of the publishers, or in the case of reprographic reproduction in accordance with the terms of licences issued by the Copyright Licensing Agency. Enquiries concerning reproduction outside those terms should be sent to the publishers.

ISBN 1 899293 29 9

Cover and illustrations: Ronald Stein

Photographs of doves kindly supplied by
Rupert Stephenson (Rupert@rupert-fish.co.uk)

Typeset in 13pt Garamond by Troubador Publishing Ltd, Market Harborough, UK

Matador
12 Manor Walk, Coventry Road
Market Harborough, Leics LE16 9BP, UK
Tel: (+44) 1858 468828 / 469898
Email: matador@troubador.co.uk
Web: www.troubador.co.uk/matador

Matador is an imprint of Troubador Publishing Ltd

"Search your Heart for
the best you can give.

Love and Light will
Show you the way"

Agnes Freeman

"Nothing rules Love,
and Love rules all things"

Anon

CONTENTS
PART ONE

Foreword		x
Acknowledgements		xi
1.	MEDIUMSHIP	1
2.	SALT & WATER MEDITATION	8
3.	TRANCE – SITTINGS & MEDIUMSHIP	10
4.	THE SPIRITUALIST APPROACH TO LIFE AFTER DEATH	13
5.	PSYCHIC ABILITY	15
6.	PSYCHOMETRY & ITS DEVELOPMENT	17
7.	PSYCHOMETRY AND OBJECT READING	23
8.	PSYCHOMETRY WITH OBJECTS – ITS HISTORY AND BACKGROUND	26
9.	TESSOMANCY – LINKING WITH THE EARTH	28
10.	DOODLES	29
11.	PARAPHERNALIA – TOOLS	31
12.	THE TAROT – YOUR WAY AND MINE	32
13.	EVP – VOICE PHENOMENON	34
14.	FLOWER, CLAIRSENTIENCE, OR FLOWER READING	35
15.	PSYCHIC ART	38
16.	HEALING SPIRITUAL HEALING	39
17.	MANTRAS – AND HEALING – THE VOICE	44
18.	REMOTE VIEWING	46
19.	ALL MEDIUMS WORK DIFFERENTLY	49
20.	THE SPIRITUAL APPROACH	52

21.	TELEKINESIS Or Moving Objects from a Distance	56
22.	THE PENDULUM	58
23.	PENDULUM READING	60
24.	ARE YOU A PSYCHIC? Could You Be a Medium?	66
25.	POTENTIALITY	68
26.	THE GRIEVING PROCESS	74
27.	REINCARNATION	77
28.	REALISATION – THE OTHER SIDE	79
29.	BACK TO EARTH, HAUNTINGS	80
30.	RESCUE – CIRCLES	82
31.	HOPE, CHARITY, KARMA Development	83
32.	CHARITY	85
33.	DEVELOPMENT	86
34.	QUESTIONS OFTEN ASKED OF MEDIUMS	93
35.	TWO SIDES TO ALL THINGS	95
36.	PSYCHIC ATTACK Psychic Protection	96
37.	AFFIRMATIONS	97
38.	TO LIVE BY THE BOOK	103
39.	HOW TO SIT WITH A MEDIUM	108
40.	A MEDIUM CANNOT BE EVERYBODY'S MEDIUM	112
41.	HOW TO SEE A SPIRITUAL HEALER What to Expect?	112
42.	PSYCHIC OR TRANCE HEALER	114
43.	THE ETHERIC	118
44.	WHAT IF?	119
45.	WHILE ON EARTH	120
46.	THE DIFFERENCE BETWEEN A PSYCHIC AND A SPIRITUALIST MEDIUM	122
47.	AND NOW WHAT ARE YOU DREAMING ABOUT?	123
48.	SPIRITUAL MEDIUMSHIP	125
49.	FURTHER TIPS ON COMMUNICATION	130
50.	MEDIUMS AIM HIGHER	136

51.	THE WAY OF LIFE	137
52.	A MEDIUM'S MOTTO SHOULD BE	138
53.	THE SEVEN LEVELS OF CONCIOUSNESS ON THE SPIRIT SIDE	139
54.	VISUALISATION	143
55.	KNOWLEDGE	146
56.	ASTRAL TRAVEL	148
57.	MUSIC IN THE PSYCHIC SENSE	150
58.	ANGELS, ANGEL CARDS	153
59.	LEARN TO BE MORE OUTGOING	167
60.	ELECTROMAGNETIC FIELDS	170
61.	AWAKENING	175
62.	THE POWER OF THE MIND	178
63.	DEATH	180
64.	THOUGHT-OGRAPHY	183
65.	EPILOGUE	189
66.	APPENDIX – FINAL WORDS	191

PART TWO

CHARLIE
A Story of a Spiritual Life **by AGNES FREEMAN**   197

Our Life is an Open Book   But We Write the Pages!

FOREWORD

AGNES FREEMAN is an Internationally well known Medium and Psychic and Animal Healer.

This is her Second Book. Her First Book was published in 2001, called *They Walk Beside Me*, available from Psychic News Ltd. (ISBN 0 –7212-0982-3).

In this book, she shows you the way how to achieve your goals, and how to learn to become a Psychic Medium with Dedication.

She is honest, forthright in her approach in a simple, easy to understand language. She works in England and in the United States, giving Survival Evidence that Life is for all ETERNITY, and you cannot die for the Life of You!

Bon Voyage, have a Good One!

ACKNOWLEDGEMENTS

My grateful thanks to Rosanna and Ronald, who helped,
with great dedication,
to transcribe and edit this book.

And thanks go to my Helpers in
the Higher Life who helped me
to make this book a reality,
including my Parents,
and all who reside in the Spirit Side,
and all those who I have loved and lost,
but not forever . . . .
because Life is EVERLASTING!

Thank you, dear readers,
For wanting to Learn
and open your heart and mind to it.

CHAPTER 1

MEDIUMSHIP

Mediumship is the Highest form of Psychic Development. One becomes a fully fledged Medium only when all the Chakras (energy centres), seven in the body, are all fully opened up.

Mediumship is also the Highest form of Spirit communication, Mind to Mind – Spirit to Spirit – Soul to Soul.

The Mental Kind, is a Mind Communication of Clairsentience.

A Clairsentient Medium feels every feeling which the deceased person has felt. It is mainly working with the Sense Perception – clear feelings. It is a very valid form of feeling and sensing, just knowing all and what the Spirit Communicator is wanting to say.

I   CLAIRVOYANCE

The Clairvoyant is able to see clearly Spirit Persons and can describe past, present and, possibly, future events (which is called Precognition).

Precognition is being clearly able to see future events as each unfolds.

The Clairaudiant is the one who can hear a Spirit very clearly as if from outside, or very clearly in one's own mind.

II CLAIRGUSTIENCE

To be able to smell clearly sharp smells of, say, tobacco, or that very special scent which the Person has loved while on Earth is quite easy for Spirit People to pick up on, and then communicate this particular manifestation vividly to the enquirer. But not their thoughts. The thought needs the Medium who is attuned to the Spirit Side and picks up the vibrations clearly, by listening to them.

A Medium is always a Special Person because he or she has dedicated their lives to it. To be a clear and good instrument for a Spirit, one has to be highly sensitive and fully attuned to the higher vibration from the Spirit World.

Good Health is essential, and a normal lifestyle, good food, rest, and now and then, a few early nights. To be a vegetarian, I believe, is a bonus. How can you work for a Spirit if your body is heavy and weighed down by meat, which takes 9–24 hours to digest properly. You cannot work if your stomach rumbles, or digestive disorders are bothering you. A great deal of water is required to get rid of all unwanted food matter.

Mediumship is an Art – or Art Form, to be perfected. You meet all kinds of people, from all walks of life, some are very sceptical, others are very open. If you can handle all the strain and all the stresses well, then you will be good instrument for Spirits. One has to work on oneself all the time to perfect it.

First of all, ask yourself why you want to be a Medium. A very honest answer is needed here in the first instance. If you come up with the right answer, and for the right reasons, go for it. It is not easy to be a good and honest Medium at all times. If you don't get any link, be honest enough to admit it, but don't give up whatever happens, if you are doing it for the right reason. Your Mediumship will flow and flourish, and you will be a good, decent instrument for Spirits who will use you; always ask the Spirit for more, it is all there for the asking. Mind you, they only give you what they do want to give you, no more and no less. If someone in the physical body while on Earth was not a good Communicator, he or she is just the same on the other side.

What they do there on the other side is not your concern, or how they progress. You are a Medium, you have to give survival evidence, first and foremost. Your job is to make sure all messages find their way home.

It takes many years of study and great patience sitting in the Circle of Development to become a Medium. Once you have achieved that, you are still wearing an "L" Plate, and will carry on wearing it until your departure from this side.

Your Job as a fully-fledged medium is to give love and light for those who otherwise have stayed in the dark. Think of yourself as a torchbearer showing the way to the Light, that life is not ending here. It is an ongoing process and we all live Forever in the Kingdom of God we call the Spirit World, where all communications originate. All animals also survive physical death, and all survive and can communicate with us!

Those of you who have read my first book *They Walk Beside Me* should know that we work with Guides. My Guides are "White Feather" and "Zohar", and a Chinese Healing Guide "Yan-zee", whom I have painted. I have seen him. No Medium works without Guides, who are the translators, interpreters, helpers, mentors, and friends from the World of the Spirit, and they are very important. When you are ready for the work you will have your Guides beside you, always. Remember, though, as you grow and change spiritually, Guides do change. Some remain in your Aura; others take their leave, so new ones can appear to help you more in your work to help others. Mediumship has to be simple and effective, to hit the nail on the head in the first few minutes when you start to open your mouth. Mediums are human beings, it is true, but Mediums with a conscience should not be a rarity, it should be a normality.

Spirit Communication is Opening the Door to the Spirit World mainly, and letting the Spirit, not yourself, do the rest. Mediumship is a very Natural Phenomenon, not Paranormal, just Supranormal. I always say try harder to be the best instrument, ask more to get more, and just deliver the undiluted message; that is all that is asked of you as a Medium.

We have had great mediums in the past, Gordon Higginson, and Albert Best (the finest). Mediums are usually born, not made, but, with total dedication, you can enhance your inborn ability, which is your Birthright. We are all Psychic to a certain extent, but to be a good Medium needs total control of all your abilities, and control with the Spirit.

You have to learn to Open the Door and also to Shut it. You have to be ready. When the Spirit makes its appearance, it is ready to communicate to loved ones, either clairvoyantly or clairaudiently. When the pupil is ready, the master appears. So, if you feel Mediumship is for you, please do go for it!

You will find some exercises to practice as well.

III HOW TO SIT FOR SPIRIT COMMUNICATION

Exercise No 1 – Called Counting Your Breath

Breath is Life!

Count for 3 seconds.

Hold for 3.

Let out for 3.

Deep, deep breath down to the solar plexus (stomach area).

And visualise a Golden Circle of Light around you, ask for the White Light of protection, and for your Guide to come closer.

If you do not know your Guide yet, do not worry, you will in good time – their time, naturally…. and not yours. Sit in a very comfortable chair, which should be straight-backed, hands on your knees, palms down, or on your thighs, whichever seems more comfortable every day at the same time. Once a week is recommended for the beginners on the journey. Advanced souls can meditate before a sitting or service takes place. Do not try to force things to happen. You can hold a small white crystal in your hand if that helps you. Flowers or cut flowers are very helpful in this atmosphere, to elevate you and to put yourself into the right frame of mind.

The sitting should be not more than 15 minutes, to begin with; you will find later, that you can lengthen the time to a 30 minute period, but not any longer than that, if you are sitting alone for development. It should be cosy, but not overwarm. You need the air to circulate – you do not want to fall asleep, you are sitting in development for Spirit mode. If your shoes bother you, take them off. Comfort is important. You must breathe naturally, close your eyes and keep them closed. Feel your breath. It will get easier as time goes by. Repeat the breathing exercise 10 times.

Exercise No 2 – To See Inwardly

Look around the room where you want to sit for development, and take in as much as you can, a picture on the wall, books, – memorise what they look like, close your eyes, take another look, take in the shapes – close your eyes, try to see with your inner eye the TV set – breathe deeply, hold your breath for a count of three. Visualise the whole room where you are sitting in, the chair on which you are sitting. See yourself sitting on that chair. That is difficult, but you will succeed. Give it another try; do not get upset or angry, eventually you will see yourself outside your body, looking at yourself.

Exercise No 3 – The Clock

See the clock, look at the numbers. See the second hand moving. Close your eyes – take a deep, deep breath at the count of three. Hold for three, let out for three.

With your eyes shut, see the second hand ticking away. See it twice, going to the 12 position – visualise 12, then 6. Open your eyes. Take a deep breath, have a good stretch upwards with your hands, like "I want to be tall". Close the exercise.

Repeat another time the same exercise until you see the

12. Stop on that for a second, then stop on 6 for a second.

A deep stretch upwards and a big yawn helps.

Further towards Realisation/Meditation

Light a white and purple candle. Take in the white light, look into the flame and keep looking until your eyes water.

Take that flame into your Third Eye (pituitary gland) located between or rather over your eyes in between the beginning of your nose.

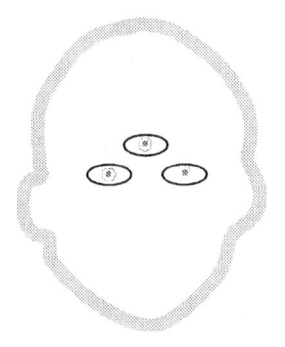

You will see that light clearly with your eyes shut. Keep practising – practice will make perfect!

Repeat the same procedure with the purple candle (not at the same time).

Look into the light, breathe in deeply to take the light to your third eye, mentally push it to open your third eye.

Keep practising!

Our Life is an Open Book   **But We Write the Pages!**

CHAPTER 2

SALT AND WATER MEDITATION

Sit in a comfortable chair, place some sea salt into a small dish on your right hand side. On your left, put a small bowl of water.

Put the fingers of your right hand into the salt and the fingers of your left hand into the water and say:

'I am connected to the Universe.'

'I am a Child of the Cosmos.'

'I am centered, and centered I stay.'

Breathe deeply, count for 10 inwards – breathe, hold as long as you can. Repeat:

'I am Centered.'

'I am Alive. I am Me.'

Ask God to allow your Guides to come. Keep still – breathe deeply and slowly.

Soft, New Age music is very helpful, played very low in the background. Then you may possibly start to experience some sensation, feelings, drifting of consciousness to a higher level. Stay as long as you feel comfortable with it. You will know when you have had enough.

Discomfort is not helpful in that kind of development. **DO NOT TRY TOO HARD!** Make sure you will not be disturbed.

CHAPTER 3

TRANCE – SITTINGS & MEDIUMSHIP

This is a very different area of development, and **you must proceed with CAUTION. Please do not do it ALONE**.

Sit in a very comfortable chair, and start breathing deeply, very deeply. Someone should watch you, but should not touch you, as this may cause a severe shock.

Be very calm and collected. Ask for your Guide to attend, pray, say the Lord's prayer which is recommended, or any prayer you like, and feel protected by it.

Have a tape recorder running, but do not force things to happen. If you try many times, and nothing happens for a long time – you are not a physical Medium, but before you give up, join a Physical Circle to see if they want you to develop that way. It is not your choice, but the Spirit's. A Physical Medium has to be in very good health, well balanced, and extremely well disciplined.

On the day before the sitting commences, eat nothing, drink nothing except WATER, to leave the physical body clean, and do have a bath or shower before you sit for that kind of development. If nothing happens, you still learn disciplineship. This is the most important requirement to be a Medium of any kind.

Nowadays, there are very few physical mediums left. Some of these are able to transfigure, which means that you can recognise your loved ones on the face of the medium, which will change accordingly. Spirit hands mould the face to that of the loved one, and this is called Ectoplasm. Many outstanding mediums have worked that way before.

Another form is DIRECT VOICE, which belongs to physical mediumship. We had in Britain the world famous Leslie Flint, and no one else has followed his footsteps.

Now there is only mental mediumship, and there are very few who are direct voice mediums, if any, the world over. Yes, we do have John Edward, the brilliant young medium in New York, USA; James van Pragh in California, and, of course, Sylvia Brownie in San Fransisco, California. She is able to find lost people, and can describe scenes of murder, giving full descriptions of people who have been involved with the murder. She is featured many times on a Cable Show hosted by Montel Williams. John Edward is always able, and very capable of linking up with Spirit Personalities, giving names all the time, places, and all the circumstances which have led to the physical death, giving the 100% survival evidence, which is what life after death, or what spiritualism stands for.

I have been to Canada, to Ontario and Toronto, visiting two churches. The services have been quite good, starting with healing, and the medium went to everybody in the congregation. The Reverend came from California. The Florida Casadega Spiritualist Camp was a quite good experience as well. The services were very different from those in England. In all fairness, I must say some were better than others, the mediums working there were honest and good. In Orange County, Florida, I took over one of the evening services, again giving good survival evidence and a dog called Sandy, a lovely labrador, made her appearance too. It is very enlightening to work in overseas churches, in a completely different and electric atmosphere, always that feeling of expectation before the service, the serene atmosphere. The singing and the candles I found very conducive for the spirit. Australia is an up and coming country, which is spiritually starved, as it were. It is a pleasure to give Enlightenment and show the Way towards the Light, especially in Melbourne. Those who seek the Light usually find it. "Man does not live by bread alone" – we all need the Spiritual Fruit to ripen. Our seven principles – nine in the USA – keep us going and aiming higher. The Spiritual Philosophy is just as important as our message services. In the USA an all message service is conducted in one of the Casadaga spiritualist churches, near Orlando, and that is also good for serving the whole purpose and ethic of the true belief.

Our Life is an Open Book   But We Write the Pages!

CHAPTER 4

THE SPIRITUALIST APPROACH TO LIFE AFTER DEATH

The Spiritualist approach towards life after physical death is a very simple one, and the simplest of things are the most important. Our approach to physical life is such that we believe that Life is for the Living to learn all lessons here and now; so when we get to the other side of life, we can view the whole picture of our earthly life, which we left behind, as something which was not completely wasted.

We know there is a Higher Life, which we call the Spirit World. We know we all survive physical death. We know we will meet up with loved ones on the other side of the veil. We know we just cross over, viewing it as the Other Side of the Bridge.

We know all our loved ones are very close to us always. We know the Human Spirit has to evolve and progress here and now, and when we cross over, especially, we know there is life after death, and we know life is Personal Responsibility, which is one of our seven principles. Life is Eternal, and we do go on Forever, once we have returned to the other side, where there is our real home. But the progress goes on. Some of us become Spirit Guides or helpers for others this side of life. Others stay there, and do the things they always wanted to do, but who had no time or opportunity to do so here. ETERNAL PROGRESS is open to all

Souls, which is our other principle well worth your thought, dear reader.

As we keep saying, "You cannot die for the Life of you." All of us were created forever and we all go on to Infinity. That is the simple TRUTH, but a very worthwhile one. If only all of you would know and realise that, you could all live your lives accordingly. The SEEKERS of you, seeking the TRUTH in this Life, sometimes find it eludes you, at other times you will find some of it, but not the Whole Truth, even part of it is good. The whole truth awaits you yet, so don't give up seeking your own TRUTH.

Our Life is an Open Book **But We Write the Pages!**

CHAPTER 5
PSYCHIC ABILITY

We are all psychic to a certain extent. If you have feelings about something before it happens, you have precognition, the ability or feeling about knowing the Future.

Intuition or Insight Into Oneself – Dreams are also important. Not all of these are necessarily Psychic, but if you see happenings related to future events, you are Psychic. A person approaches you, and you immediately do not like that Person.

Why should this be? There is no answer to that – either that person is not on your own psychic wavelength, or comes close to your AURA – i.e. has overstepped the Psychic Boundary, but whatever feeling you come up with, STICK to the feeling. You are usually right.

Dislike of crowds and dislike of noise. You are psychic. If you have strong feelings when you go somewhere for the first time, either you like it or dislike it very strongly. There may be smells you dislike, or smells you like. Do you really have no idea why? Because you are psychic.

All these feelings make up the 10% of your psychic self, and demonstrates that this is alive and working. When the 20% of your psychic brain abilities starts to work, the right hand side of your brain is engaged. You are beginning to have knowledge, suddenly, more so than before.

Picking up languages, even though you do not understand that language, you suddenly know what they are talking about. It is especially so if you are the topic of their conversation. Try it! Listen to people talking, you can make it out psychically. Try to understand it.

Some people do not even bother to listen to their own language, or someone talking to them. You can beat that by becoming interested in others. Open up your psychic faculties. It is amazing what you can find, and it will enrich your life. It will make you a happier, a much more open person, a nicer person – well, hopefully.

It is only 20% of your right hand brain which is working, so aim to get more. Try to reach 30%, which is better, and it will get better all the time, all the way.

Our Life is an Open Book   But We Write the Pages!

CHAPTER 6

PSYCHOMETRY AND ITS DEVELOPMENT

In Psychometry, depending on the individual, we can access the human Psyche. We see the past by touching only, or object holding. I believe metal objects are the best for that method. It depends on the Psychometrist how that person is capable of penetrating into the object! The object is you – This is your Life! This is your Vibration! This is the way you react to Life, and Life's challenges. The people you have met, will meet, and definitely link with the Spirit. Not all Psychometrists do of course. It very much depends on your own development as a fully-fledged Psychometrist. I get Spirit Communication most of the time. I get Guides known to the participant, or yet to be revealed. But important information regarding status, character, life, hobbies, even which sex the person prefers, all pours out. It is only a question how to get the right vibration from it, and the best way to go. The best way is to write down all impressions, or tape-record them, as you will not remember them a minute afterwards. It is a brilliant exercise to link up with the Higher Self and the Higher Life. To see you as a person, with all your negative and positive qualities. Be very careful if you professionally read someone. Never say anything detrimental to the character of the person you are reading. Whatever you give out has to be Positive and also uplifting so watch your negative thoughts, which may be coming through. Block them out! There is no room for Negativity.

Beside, you have to be in a positive mood to read another. You can exercise by holding any inanimate object, like a watch, a ring or keys, but they have to have been handled already by the person you are reading. Grandmother's ring, second hand, will not do! You will only pick up the wrong vibes, and the message will get mixed up. This has happened to me a few times! Luckily I have known the person has tried to trick me! I am a Psychic after all! I can't be tricked! I point out, very quickly, "Sorry – it has belonged to someone before you, or bought second hand, or someone has given you that". That way, honesty pays dividends, and the person very shamefacedly admits it, anyway. "I didn't want to trick you. Sorry! Oh yes! Aha!" Another trick has failed, so I will have the last laugh!

Not everybody is brilliant at reading another's soul that way. It works for me! You can try it, it might work for you too, with trial and error eventually it will, if you are Psychic and Sensitive to the touch Vibration.

Some people like to touch, others do not. Usually, if you are yourself a very outgoing person, and sensitive, you will surely succeed in picking up all you can from any objects. Pick up a pebble on the beach, any beach anywhere, and try to feel what that pebble is telling you. Guess it's age, what that pebble has seen as civilisations have come and gone. Who were the people who walked on it, touched it, thrown it into the sea, how did it get washed out again, and again. Try to guess whether it gave shelter to any sea creature at any time – or perhaps not!

Was it part of a bigger stone? Had it broken away? If yes, when – and how? Was it in happy times in history, or not? Had that pebble seen the Crusaders? The Vikings? Has it been around King Arthur's feet? Or even further back in time – Stone-Age? Bronze Age? Iron Age? Or is it more recent? Then try an old book from any antique shop. It is amusing what you can learn – who was the owner of that yellowing book? Was it loved? Re-read? Or did it just gather dust in a large, stately home, unloved and never read? Is the owner still alive? Who owned that book? How many people possibly handled it? What did they look like? Where have they or do they live? Are they no longer with us? Or are they still alive? Do they love life? Have they had children? Was it a child who read that book? Was it an adult? Was it a man? Was it a woman? What do they look like? What did they do for a living? Was it a hard life or a leisurely one? Do they like music? Have they played music? What was the name of the music – if any comes to mind?

The whole history of the book and the people who touched it, or were touched by it, is all in the touch of your fingertips. It is a question of picking up these vibes, and interpreting them as they come in the strong, very, very strong thought form. Feelings, or sounds in your ear even. You can Psychometrise anything. Do take your time – to get excellent results you will have to learn and re-learn a lot. It is a different concept of Psychic Reality. You can be brilliant, or you can be very mediocre with it. Aim for the highest to get the best results – 10 out of 10. It is in your own interest to be the best – I mean the best in whatever you do – you might as well do it properly. It makes sense not to settle for less. Many Psychics are working on an extremely low level. Perhaps they never bother to learn to work for the highest good. To be mediocre in anything won't do you or any others any good! Only the best will do – please do remember that, dear reader, or student of the Paranormal, as they say in the U.S.A. metaphysical studies.

Be yourself. "Let go – Let God!" What a very wise super saying that is. Did it really originate in the Bible? Is every religion believing something of that kind? All I know is that in a spiritual way we say "Yes, not me." Let go of suffering Negative energy. Let God, or the Higher Power, the Great Spirit of the Universe, the White Light, sort out your problems.

When you feel you need help – we all do sometimes – close your eyes and ask, not necessarily pray in any orthodox sense of religion of any kind. Create your own! Why not? Whatever you believe in is good for yourself. The Universe, Spirit World or Eternity – all are the same. It is fine – it keeps you alert, Positive, and keeps you ticking over. Even a clock needs oiling sometimes – so do you. So whatever makes you think is fine and O.K. to the Higher Forces, who are watching your faltering steps – for sure – and do help if you ask for it.

You remember when you were a child, you had to ask your mother or father for things you wanted. Well, you're a big, overgrown child now, and you have earthly needs, so why don't you ask? Your father or mother were no mind-readers either. The same applies to the Higher Forces – ask, so you shall be given. (I have to add – if they seem to fit you). It might not serve the higher purpose, but it is what your over-soul needs. So be it!

Ask for more knowledge – and please cultivate self-knowledge. "Physician know thyself!" Yes please! When you understand who you are, and what you are, then only you can go and help others.

Understanding begins with oneself, first and foremost, and always. Be clever, be kind to yourself, do yourself a big favour and love yourself. Then only you can love and understand others too.

It makes sense. Common-sense.

So we have got to the point that you are a Psychic, and you are using your God-given ability. Good! Learn that violin and how to play it properly! Use your Psychic senses, and aim to be a virtuoso.

I know that even if you can play the piano not all make it to the concert platform, but you can try! "A job well done" should ring in your ears.

Enthusiasm makes a big difference, and you have to feel it, you cannot learn it in the College of Psychic Studies. You are guaranteed you cannot learn it from sitting in a circle for Psychic Development.

Either you have it, or you have not got it, and, if you have not, no one on Earth can put that in you.

Be enthusiastic – you are a Psychic, and should see things clearer than any one else, in theory. Without enthusiasm what is left? An empty shell! Do remember that.

You are a seer – for others.

You are the pointer for others.

You have got to be stronger than others mentally, and don't neglect your physical body either. Clean that body twice daily, at least – you will feel better and work better. And, of course, I cannot emphasise the importance of the right diet.

It should be pure food, not animal, not flesh of any kind. If you like, you can have fish. Fish is a brain food – yes! Any or oily fish, such as sardines, are good for your mind and your body too. But all in moderation. A Psychic has to be a fit human being. Plenty of water is needed for mind/body maintenance. You need the sun, and you need the moon. You need to rest your busy mind. A good night's sleep is essential to all sentient beings.

Observe a cat. It knows when it has had enough, and just curls up and has a lovely dream. What do cats dream about – who knows?

Animal Psychology

Animal Healing and Animal Behaviour Therapy. It all belongs to that sphere of activity if you're a pet psychic (which I am).

I know what they do dream about. Some dreams are of a lovely partner, others are about their favourite food. Good old pussy might also dream about the pain in its upper tooth.

What do dogs dream about? A big bone! A lovely run in the park! The neighbour's dog as a friend or partner. A better bed to sleep on. The love they are missing.

CHAPTER 7
PSYCHOMETRY

Object Reading

Every inanimate object gives out a certain vibration. Ask a friend to give you his or her watch. Hold it in your hand for a second or two. You will then be reading the object. You are reading the person to whom that object belongs. Try to feel it for a few seconds only. Whatever comes to mind, give it out quickly. You cannot go very far wrong.

You possibly pick up names, places, what he or she does workwise – that is, when you have never met the person previously. Here are some questions you will be wanting to find the answers for: Car, ask mentally has he or she a car: What colour, what make? Try to see the registration number (Remote Viewing) Many times you will see or hear from people on the Spirit Side. This means that the person you are reading has a Helper, relatives, dogs, cats, pet birds, parrots or whatever comes. But do not try too hard. Let it flow, flow is important.

At first, do not try to make any sense of whatever comes, category arrives at a later date. Try to see the place where the person lives, works, ambition, past, present and future, health and wealth. For instance, can you see a ring? Is the person going to get married, and if so, when. (Timing is difficult). Then there are moves, changes in the person's life. Are there any pets, or were there some in the past? Did the pet go away and return? Try to read the person's aptitudes, what is he or she best at doing, should be doing, going to do, or not. Do not forget free will, this is personal choice.

Does the person have anyone in the Spirit World? Do not go back too far if the person is too young, since he or she will probably not know anything about them, in all probability. Close family ties . . . . names, if any come up.

Special interests? If there are any hobbies? What that person is best at doing, or should be doing.

Inner thoughts, wishes, any future events?

Psychometry and Missing Persons

Do not forget Psychometry is a tool which you can use to discover missing people, or missing pets with.

If someone comes to you with some belongings of that person –the one who is seeking – impressions will come to your mind, and it should lead you there, where the person can be found – hopefully.

The best thing is to write down whatever you get, or if you are holding the object, let the person who came to consult you write it down. You are busy with your own mind. You will receive personal traits and facial characteristics, what the person looked like, felt like, where he/she used to go, places, friends, relatives and what happened to the person.

For example, I had someone who was looking for a missing parrot.

I called at the house, held the cage which housed the parrot. I then got a street name; a dog, two children and a lady will open the door; they have a very large garden, and a huge sheep dog. We drove around to the house, and found the place in Finchley on the outskirts of London, England. The lady opened the door. The large, friendly sheepdog, ran out. I told them, "I am a psychic and a parrot is in your garden." By that time, the lady's husband had appeared. I said, "Yes, it is up in the trees, and talking". We went out to the garden, accompanied by the lady of the house, her husband, their 11-year old daughter, and 13-year old son, and the sheepdog. The lady, who was the owner of the parrot, and her 10-year old daughter, and 14-year old son came with me. We found the parrot. We kept calling him, but that parrot thought the better of it, and flew away!

I wonder what became of the parrot, a talking parrot in a cold British winter. Why did it not come down: and why did it fly away? Who knows? All I know is that I did find it. So can you!

Our Life is an Open Book   But We Write the Pages!

CHAPTER 8

PSYCHOMETRY WITH OBJECTS: ITS HISTORY AND BACKGROUND

You can hold any object and try to go back in time with it. Feel the place where it was made, and where it has been, or made, or whether it is natural, what is its habitat, if it is a crystal or stone, or even a fossil. Try to feel its country of origin. Keep going back in time to when it was formed, what kind of people touched it, what was the use of that object?

Who was the original owner? You can get names, places, even years, since we are going back in time. Ask yourself is it B.C.?, A.D.? How far back in time is that object taking me? If it is a historical artefact of some kind, go back in time, and see what you get.

Handling second-hand antique objects always gives me shivers up and down my spine. Mind, that depends where that particular object has come across its time. The people who handled it, loved it. The joy it caused, or the pain or hatred it created by parting with it. An old table can talk to you and tell you a most interesting story. Its history, all is imprinted in it. A stone from the beach can talk to you just as much as the Crown Jewels, and a single stone can tell you quite a revelatory story as well.

Whenever you handle old objects, always ask that question, how does it feel? Am I happy with it? Unhappy?

Or neither here or there. Is it important? Unimportant? Relevant? Or is it irrelevant? **Trust** your feelings, go after it. **Trust that object in your hand.** Many things will come to mind, sort it out later on.

Think about it. You dig up a garden and you find an old coin. Hold it in your hand, and it will possibly tell you the story of the owner who lived in that house before. What they were like, were they pleased with their life? Was there peace in the home, or arguments? Had it been modernised? All that from an old farthing!

CHAPTER 9

TESSOMANCY – LINKING WITH THE EARTH

Sand Reading – Tea-Leaf Reading

If you are clairvoyant, which you definitely need to be for that particular subject, Sand Reading is a very ancient art, originating from ancient Egypt. All you need is fresh, virgin sand from any beach, a large tray and then shake up the sand. For the person for whom you are reading, that person should put their hand in it, do what they like with it. In a childlike playful way, just disturb the sand, and when the person has finished with it, you take a closer look.

What shapes do you see in the sand? Do you see any initials? PAST, PRESENT, FUTURE. Perhaps a musical instrument? And what does that thing suggest to you in connection with that person? Whatever you do see, give out Faces, Places. I do see Spirit Guides in it, so can you, if you really look to see.

CHAPTER 10
DOODLES

Not so much in the psychic, but the psychological you. Whatever you doodle, if you do this at all, it has a meaning for you. When a psychic or psychologist analyses your artwork, they usually come up with somewhat similar explanations. **A tree** without leaves is not a good sign. The way you are feeling about life and yourself, you are that tree. **A tree** is an essence, and the essence of life, your back, your spinal column, the very you is that tree. Basic instinct, bereavement, lethargy, depression, winter, all those feelings link with it.

The more elaborate your tree is drawn, full of springy tangly leaves, full grown, that is you again, you have found yourself, have found your roots and the branches are you again. The leaves signify achievement in your life.

Circles – you are running round in circles.

Flowers of any kind – This means something coming to flower, flourishing, achievements, possibly names linking with it. Violets are wisdom. Margaritas – can be an initial M. Roses – mean celebration, happiness, and achievement. Faces – you are wishing to express yourself in some way.

House – you are insecure, you are wishing for a better

place or abode, depending on the kind of house you have drawn. The taller the house, the more you are wishing for it to come about.

People – stick people like matchsticks. It is people generalisation – they have become all the same to you, meaning you have given up, living a robot-like existence.

Circle within a circle – You are really stuck in life, and you cannot see any way out.

Snakes – venom – a bad feeling, or you do not like orthodox medicine. On the other hand, you might be dealing with it, but not liking it.

Trains – you want to get away – not so fast!

Boats – slow down, you need a brake on life.

Many lines – you are up and down like a yo-yo.

CHAPTER 11
PARAPHERNALIA – TOOLS

Crystal Balls – projecting outward, look into the ball.

What do you see? Your own reflection? Nothing at all?

Do not eat, or have a very light meal only – every night at the same time. Sit quietly, have a candle at arm's length at least, look into the ball.

At first, you will see nothing at all, but, by trying, it will reveal itself to you, what you are asking for, if you are clairvoyant outwardly.

I call it a **PROJECTION OF THOUGHTS**. You might see or feel – it is only to focus on. Don't let your eyes **WATER**. Take it in easy steps for a maximum of 10 minutes. Keep trying. Don't give up – if you have tried for a month, and you felt nothing, saw nothing, it is not for you – so go for something else. After all, it is a tool only, or a focal point.

Find your own way about to what really suits your needs.

Our Life is an Open Book   But We Write the Pages!

CHAPTER 12

THE TAROT – YOUR WAY AND MINE

There are hundreds of different Tarot packs available. You have to find the one you really like, and would like to work with.

Start by looking at the pictures, every card tells a story – don't read the instruction booklet.

Put out just six cards. (Don't read for yourself.) Try to tell a friend what you feel, see, experience. Any question? And can you answer it?

Add three cards for the answer. You draw them, not the enquirer.

Many books have been written about the Tarot, all are unique in their own way.

The Truth is that you must find your own way around it. It can be bewildering at first, but soon you will get used to the feelings of handling the CARDS, not shuffling them to death. I don't believe in shuffling for a very long time, but find your own way, do not do it for fun, be serious about it, about what you want to achieve, and don't read the TAROT for yourself, it is not a Toy! Be studious, be serious, and it will give up its secrets to you, to help others.

The Fledglings Way to Mediumship

Your chosen CARDS need to be protected, always put them away, and nobody but you is allowed to handle them. Take care with it.

At first, write down all the impressions you have; practice, because practice makes perfect. Use your God-given intuition, you need to be intuitive in the first case.

Use your inner knowledge – you already have that. It is only a question of tapping into your Inner Self, Higher Self, Inner Ability.

YOU WILL SUCCEED!

Use your Tarot intuitively – Success will follow. You will be blessed with knowledge. Do it the Right Way. Energy follows Thought.

Do it for the Right Reason, and you will be blessed with success!

CHAPTER 13

EVP – VOICE PHENOMENON

You can capture Spirit Voices on tape. Keep your tape recorder running all night, the auto-reverse function is essential!

I have tried many times and only once have I heard a faint hallo sound, but it does not mean you might be luckier to try it and get good results. Do not give up. You do need a good microphone, too, and first-class audio-tape.

It is not one of my favourite ways to communicate with Spirits, but then again, I am not a Physical Medium – not generating energy to feed that particular kind of phenomenon.

They make their presence felt anyway. I feel that they find it difficult to find the physical voice, and by thought alone to transfer it onto the tape. They found that easier a long time ago, and with the Right Physical Instrument, that type of medium, with a Direct Voice, one to express their earthly Voice – and only the great Leslie Flint Brittain was the best Physical medium to produce that particular type of Phenomenon.

CHAPTER 14

FLOWER CLAIRSENTIENCE, OR FLOWER READING

Flower reading has been with us for quite some time. People love to give flowers – we get flowers (our mothers do) when we are born. We get flowers for Birthdays. We send flowers for Anniversaries. We send flowers to the sick – it has a healing effect.

We get flowers when we get married and, lastly, we get flowers when we die. So flowers are with us all our Earth Lives. The Spirit World is also full of flowers – but they never die, never wilt, they live forever, and they shine out to their full glory and AURA.

I love to do flower readings. First of all, flowers are beautiful, and they speak to us in their own symbolical language. When I carry out a flower reading, I have a very large bunch of all kinds, so that people whom I will read later have a choice.

Why people choose some flowers and not others, is because they have their own particular reason for it. I recommend a Rose, a Red Rose always reminds you of a loved one, or the very rose you put on a loved one's grave, perhaps.

LILIES – you have made a good choice, not just the purity and the fragrance and their immense beauty, but probably the very name, Heidi, Lillian, Lill have a meaning for you. I tell people to hold their chosen flower for as long as I allow them. Then I hold it – and the Spirit always comes through to communicate and to validate, to send their love to you, and to give you that much needed SURVIVAL EVIDENCE. The Human Spirit survives physical death, so do all Animals.

I get names, dates, and places with your flower, it is a lovely way to link up with a Spirit. They love flowers in the Higher World as well. You too can easily try it. Examine the essence of that flower, the leaves, and the stem. Is it small? Is it tall? Count the leaves, if possible. It possibly has a meaning for the One who has chosen that particular flower you are working with in your Mind and Spirit senses, hence the name Flower – Clairsentience, I love it!

Flowerclairsentience and Clairaudience work hand in hand. You sense very clearly, then hear clairaudiently as well. I do, so can you. It is a question of practising it. You can tape-record your sessions even while you are practising. Don't worry, the Spirit World wants you to work for them, but you must search your own heart diligently, why you want to be a Medium. Mediumship can be a blessing, but at all times, it is a heavy responsibility also. Don't forget that!

The way you deliver your messages is your responsibility, not to add to it, no padding, just the flow is needed, your attunement to the Spirit's Higher Vibration. The better the Person you become, the better you will be the better Instrument to the Spirit. Always aim higher. In that way, only the best will come to you, clear undiluted Spirit Communication, the very evidence of Survival – to give, and you can only do that if your mind is on Higher Things, if you are a good, honest Person.

TRUTHFULNESS is my first Principle, beside our Seven

Principles. It is not easy to be a Medium, even so, it seems so easy. Your attunement to the Higher Vibratory rate makes it so. Simplicity is the very best key to it.

Tom Johanson, the ex-President of the Spiritualist Association of Great Britain, has told me that. His wonderful wife was the most famous Coral Polge, the amazing Psychic Artist. I treasure her drawing of my grandmother, and her name was also given out by the Medium. She was not only a brilliant psychic Artist, but a Good Medium as well.

Our Life is an Open Book   But We Write the Pages!

CHAPTER 15

PSYCHIC ART

A Psychic Artist is a person who is able to link visually with Spirit Personalities and able and capable of drawing them clearly, so that people can recognise departed relatives. All kinds of human beings come through, as well as all kinds of animals. This includes Guides and Helpers, your very own ones; Guardian Angels, not relatives. Your Helper, your Doorkeeper, your Mentor, these all come through, if summoned. It is wonderful to work with a psychic artist on the stage. I worked with Nick Ashron, and he delivered very fast drawings; and I have linked up with the picture, giving survival evidence, and other mediums can work with you as well. It is nice for the audience or congregation to see different kinds of Mediumship, working side by side, and loved ones as drawn.

One of these successful evenings was in Eastbourne, East Sussex. This is a pleasant place to work in, lovely people, all eager to hear from departed, loved ones. And the drawings were done as very good survival evidence to take home with them, a souvenir from the Other Side, given with great love for people residing on This Side of the Vale. They are only a thought away and love never dies. They come when they are needed; where there is a great need, they are aware of it.

CHAPTER 16

SPIRITUAL HEALING

Many are called, but few are chosen. A Healer is born a Healer, but then again, you can attune yourself with your Helpers, your Spirit Guides, who were doctors on the Earth Plane, not all of them however, and they will stand with you, while you do the healing.

It is not Faith Healing, neither is it Reiki nor Crystal Healing.

It is Spiritual Healing, which comes from God's Country, and we are working with the Guides we will get to know at a later date. It usually takes two years to develop one's abilities as a Healer, and this is a serious business, being a Healer.

You cannot work from the solar plexus area – you become ill, so mainly one has to learn to keep calm with all kinds of people; kind, but not over-kind, otherwise you get ill. You must not take on other people's ailments and illnesses. You must learn to stand still, to be still. Let God and the Guides guide and protect and heal the person, or whatever animal you are healing through God and your Spiritual Helpers. This is a form of Mediumship. We call that the Healer-Medium, there is no better word for it.

You don't need to be a Saint or a Martyr. You simply

need to be a strong, capable and down-to earth person who can heal and are able to help; with the help of your Guides, of course.

I have a Chinese Healer Guide, and the long departed HARRY EDWARDS (the world famous Healer in England before the last war) helps me now and then. He was the only Healer in the whole world who was capable of filling the Royal Albert Hall completely – there was only standing room left!

Another was DORIS STOKES, but she was also a Medium, very well liked, a popular, grandmotherly type lady. Healing should be made simple, no ceremony, as the Guides do the work. Etiquette is important. The Code of Conduct must be learned and learned well.

One Golden Rule – Never Heal Alone, always have somebody else with you.

It is unethical to work alone with the opposite sex, this is not permitted. We have the N.F.H.S. and the W.F.H. and other healing organisations, where one can learn as a probationer. Two years is absolutely necessary. Another ingredient, diligence, steadfastness – we all get there. If your heart goes out when you see suffering, and you want to help, probably you are a healer.

You must learn to give from the heart, or wanting to give for very little, or no return at all, except a thank-you, if you are lucky enough to get even that.

People who have been healed forget you, but when the phone rings, and someone lets you know that he or she is better, you feel very humble, very uplifted, and happy for that person. So you see it is all very worthwhile, but not for your ego. Please learn it is not you who heals, but God and the Guides.

You are only the Instrument. You might well be an important one, but still, you are you, that, and no more. A good, accomplished Healer, yes, perhaps, but please, all of you who are aiming that way, please keep yourselves humble. You are not the Healer, it comes from on high, but do your job well.

Be happy, be blessed for whatever you do to help others to alleviate any kind of suffering. All our animals need you, too.

I was in Rochester, Kent, when an elderly couple approached me with a beautiful labrador dog. I think they called him Donny. However, that dog needed healing. He was 14 year old, and he was wetting himself, and he did not like it one little bit; not to mention the owners. Initially I explain to Donny "I will not touch you, I will just inspect your body all-round, and you will feel better." He lay down, and looked up at me with huge, brown, pleading eyes, and I bent down, rather than sitting down on the floor next to him. He liked that – it was not too overpowering. "What does that big human lady want to do? She doesn't even want to touch me?" The next time I went back to Rochester he ran up to me, and lay down as before. The urinary complaints had started to clear up. The last time I went to Rochester, he greeted me with a wagging tail, and no urinary problems. He wasn't wetting himself any more, and he was very well indeed. I love success stories. Animals are so good, and ready to accept healing. I kissed him on the head. "Goodbye, be good! I love you!"

The owner of a lovely ginger cat called Ben gave me his photograph to look at and asked me to do something, as he was very ill. I held his photograph and we began to talk. I felt his little body, I felt the pain, his pain, his stomach trouble, back-pain, that he was feeling very lethargic, listless, nearly lifeless, poor thing! I sent distant healing right away, and I asked my Guides to attend to his needs. He has got much better, without seeing the vet.

Mind you, many veterinary surgeons work via the Spirit-side, with Guidance on the earth plane. There are no problems too small, or too large to help with here.

Not all ailments can be healed, that is true, but, believe me, if they are caught in time, most are, if not all. Sometimes, it is not meant to be, just like with people, and other times it is very much meant to be, so it will be done. I say "Thy will be done. For sure, and always!" We cannot reason that one out – there is no answer for it. We all suffer one time or another here!

You can never take for granted good health; in your or your animals. We all need to look after ourselves. A proper diet is necessary for healthy living. The good food Guide to your life, or for your pets, is necessary if you want to avoid ailments. Good health is the most important thing you can have, you only know that once you lose it!

The best thing to do is to take care of it. Eat properly prepared good food, mainly vegetables, and plenty of fruit and water. Your animals also need proper looking after. I would say food, love and shelter are important, but food first, love second, and shelter, which is very essential, comes last in the list. Your pets are psychic – they know your moods – and understand you very well, so you should at least try to be their best friend too – when they look at you with pleading eyes they want to tell you something. Please take a minute to listen to their needs. Spiritually too, if you listen, they can talk to you too. I know what they think, but then again, I am a pet psychic too. I love all creatures great or small – and I mean all. The snail in the garden is just as important as your beloved cat. I feel very sad, if, by not watching very carefully in the garden, I step on a poor snail by accident. I am immediately overcome by remorse afterwards, even though it was not my fault. Take very great care of what you do in this world. Kill nothing, harm no one. You can't create anything. God is the creator of all things only.

The only thing you can make here in this world is a child – you can give a body to that particular soul – but it's spirit comes from elsewhere. It's spirit comes from where we all come from, elsewhere, and where we are all going home to – the spirit world, as where all our beloved animal friends come from. I have two cats in the higher life – one of them usually comes to visit, and stays for a bit. Cats are very independent creatures. The other cat doesn't even bother to come, which shows that they still have the same temperament as they had when they left here. Nothing is changed when you enter the Spirit World, except your physical body, which you left behind. You are as you always have been, and always will be, yourself, a spirit in essence. Always remember that when you are done, or for whatever reason you become a spirit, with your body here and now, and always will be.

Our Life is an Open Book   But We Write the Pages!

CHAPTER 17

MANTRAS AND HEALING – THE VOICE

MANTRAS are important phrases to repeat time and time again. "Omma" is one of those words we often use. "Omma" signifies a link to the Universe. We can also sing the word "Aumm". You can begin in a low voice, and it should resonate a long time in your throat and chest, and you can also take it down to the solar plexus area. You can feel your stomach muscles tighten and then loosen. We can use "Omm – Omm – Omm" to heal our own body by the voice alone.

You can resonate "Aumm – Aumm – Aumm" low down and then higher up, but it is better to start higher up and drop the sound down to really resonate properly. You can tape-record it and play it back whenever you feel you need some self-help, some self-soul healing. It also helps to open up the psychic abilities too; the chakras. So 'aumm' – in every shape and form is a very important word to chant as a mantra.

I used to use the sound of 'aumm' or 'omm' a lot when I studied, and even today I use it when I feel the need for it, either for self-healing or meditation before I close my eyes. It opens one up – it clears your body – and opens the mind on the right side of the brain. Overall it is good for you. Such a simple word goes such a very long way. I use another word but it is very sacred to me, so I keep that one to myself only. If you seek to find a word that has meaning for you for self-development, find it, and use it. Your confidence will grow. It is your key to open your door of the spirit. Don't forget the door only opens when you are ready for it, have asked or begged for it, and offered plenty in return. In the meantime use the 'aumm' meditation. It is such a wonderful word to sing and resonate. Feel it, it is a feelable resonance. Try it and enjoy the power of Wisdom – the Universe – 'Aumm'.

Our Life is an Open Book   But We Write the Pages!

CHAPTER 18

REMOTE VIEWING

When I think my mind is a telescope I am able to see how or what Doris is doing in Liverpool, or Aunt Sally in Australia.

On the other hand we can use that exceptionally important tool to find criminals just by focusing on those particular persons. A photograph is helpful. I just ask my mind and my Guide's permission. "Can I do that! Can I help someone if I do that?" When I get the all-clear I go ahead with it. Always remember remote viewing is an experiment. It can be a wonderful mind-bending exercise. But not everyone can do it, not even one in two Psychics. Uri Geller does it very well! He has conducted many laboratory tests to prove that it is effective. He is the Master in this Art – very few are!

It sounds easy perhaps, but it is far from it! You have to try and try again, not giving up until you have, possibly, had some success with it.

Visualisation comes first. Secondly comes Remote Viewing. You need to give yourself a chance. A positive mood is needed when you try it.

Just think about it, you have tapped into your very own remote control device – to view a distant land –

through your very own mind. Once you have found that right button you will know you have managed it for sure!

This is the psychic phenomenon. To view via the Spirit is a Spiritual phenomenon. Very few of us have seen the Spirit World, and those of us who have been there, and have been thrown out, are here for a reason. We were given only a glimpse of it. Exit meant Out – being sent back here to do your work, and live your life, till your time is up, you have to stay here within your body.

I have had this experience. I nearly died once, and I found myself upstairs, as I call the Spirit World. Downstairs is always here and now. It is very nice upstairs, but I only had a minute's glimpse of it, of what is yet to come. I saw two beautiful shining Guides coming towards me, who promptly ushered me out. I saw the Light. I did!

We only know about the other side of life from the spirit entities, or Guides, who communicate with us from there. All of them can only give as much as they know from their particular level of understanding, no less and no more, not less and definitely not more. It is like the situation on earth when some of us have gone to University, and know more than, say, someone who has only finished their education with a couple of O or A Levels, and nothing else.

Living is learning, even breathing is a job. Walking requires body knowledge, but it is not something you have to think consciously about. Your mind tells your body how to walk… how to breathe…so no special efforts are needed on your part, except when you take a living breath consciously. That requires effort.

Sitting for the examination for the development or your

Mediumistic Abilities requires a real effort. A very great deal of that requires total dedication and total commitment. It is not the easiest of things to become a fully-fledged Medium.

We need to learn the Great Responsibility that goes with being a Spiritualist Medium, plus, I must add, total Honesty. You must also learn that it is not very easy either, to separate what Spirits are telling you (not your imagination) and to deliver that all-important message.

The person in front of you sees in you – the only medium he/she were going to see or come across – and you have to deliver at all times. The Medium can, admittedly, have an off-day – but the Spirit-People never have an off one. They are always spot-on. Be careful how you translate certain messages ... they have to be clear! They must have a meaning only to the recipient. It has to sound TRUE because it is TRUE! Do not change anything – have the honest TRUTH in your mind only, and, if in certain cases you only get a shorter message, please say so. Some people expect too much, others nothing at all, others haven't a clue what to expect. But all react the same way to the truth. The WATERWORKS get turned on – so you know you are on the Right Path, with the Right Person, and the right Spirit Communicator is with you; beside you; talking to you, and you are also able to describe Him/Her/a dog/a cat. It is that which is important!

Our Life is an Open Book   **But We Write the Pages!**

CHAPTER 19

ALL MEDIUMS WORK DIFFERENTLY

If you have ever seen two or more mediums you realise we all work very, very differently from each other.

The only thing is we all give you SURVIVAL evidence (not proof) but everyone in their very own unique style. Some are better with all names and details than others. Education Is important for a mediums, and sitters to.

If people would only know how to be a good listener it would make my job and my fellow mediums job so much better and easier to do.

Golden Rules

The most important rule is that we do not need the sitter to volunteer information. We give you what you need. You don't need to ask any questions, you will get all the answers. Do not try to lead, dear sitter, with a leading question to the Medium. Mediums do not require any questions to be put to them.

Don't offer any information, under any circumstances – just reply 'yes' or 'no'. I get all the information about animals from a Spirit guide I especially asked for. But I have also asked my Guides not to give me any murder cases or suicides, except under special conditions.

Accept what you get (that goes for the sitter) and for the Medium also.

Secondly, Impatience. Negative moods do not produce a conductive atmosphere, and can be a problem. A very hostile sitter can be a risk too, especially to your health.

I have seen some brilliant mediums working all over the world. You must bear one thing in mind – we are all at different development levels of understanding, and you can only give what you were able to comprehend yourself. And on the other hand, the Spirit knows exactly what you can give, and gives that directly to me. Foreign sentences and words are easy for me to deal with. Other Mediums however, would want everything in English, which is not always possible. The Spirit gives what it wants to give, but the Medium should be well chosen by the Spirit.

The Communicator and the Sitter

The Medium has to be well attuned to the Communicator, and the sitter's energy too. The Medium does not need the sitter's energy, but the Spirit Communicator does. No 'yes' or 'no', no communication! All mediums can still learn even more – especially when we get symbols. Symbols are very important, possibly they mean a lot to the Communicator, or it can mean, will mean, has meant something to the sitter, even though they don't remember it right now! They might realise it as soon as they get home, or even before.

A car is a good place to think over the meaning of symbols, as long as you're not the driver! The spirit might not want you to join them right now. You have to think what it means in their terminology – or meant – or will mean. It can be a mind-boggling process, but the truth is in there somewhere, in the form of a coded message, one that the recipient should only understand, especially in public demonstrations, and where privacy might be intruded upon, except by this method of coded messages.

CHAPTER 20

THE SPRITUAL APPROACH

The Spiritual approach to life is simple. Live the Spiritual Life. Help others even though it may inconvenience you many times. I believe one has to be good, and, if it isn't second nature to you yet, you have to learn this fact. Life is simple, so do try to simplify things. The Spiritual approach to life is not to hoard money, but to distribute it – make money work for you – give it away – not all of it, but give according to how much you earn. If you don't like to help other people, give to help defenceless animals. As I often say, they can't go shopping. Spiritualism is the very opposite of Materialism. We know we cannot take it with us – and you only earn good points here, and not in the Spirit World. Giving is receiving in every way. Live your life in the best possible way you can, so when departure comes – and it will to all of us – there will be no regrets, or at least very few. To live by the book is not as hard as you think, and it is really the only way to live. Be especially good to all Animals. They can't thank you for it, not being able to speak our language, but they can give you so much love back, as a very special thank-you! They actually do talk, but if you are not a Psychic you will not understand them, unfortunately. They do talk if you care just to open your heart and listen to it.

Cats can say miaow in many ways, and every mao, or miaow, means something different. My neighbour's cat called Dennis visits me very often, and says mao – I say mao back to her. She is a huge black cat, with the most beautiful golden eyes. They wanted a he cat, but it turned out to be a she, and the name stuck. So we've got Dennis – not the menace. She is angelic, and she stays many hours with me. She jumps up on my lap, but like a dog, follows me everywhere, even to the shower, staying well out of the water spray, of course. As long as she is able to see me she is happy. I have tried to give her all kinds of food, but she won't eat any of it. She must be given dry cat food to eat, and I'm sorry, but I haven't got any. She loves me nevertheless. When I talk to her she is very vocal, and I always get an answer when I ask her something. Sometimes she just says "oh, ohh" when she sees me in the garden, and if I stay there, she does too. When I leave she runs after me, and follows me up the stairs. She knows where I live, and there is no mistake about which door she stops at. Sometimes she sits on my lap and puts her paws around my neck. That's what I call "I love you truly!" She really does! Cats know if you're a good person and come to you, being so very Psychic, and if they avoid someone like the plague, that person is no good, and you should avoid them, likewise. Cats can feel how you were feeling – they know! Dogs know too! They really read you like a book, and your mood swings are second nature to them. If you are happy or sad watch how your animal come closer to you, especially if you're feeling down or ill. If you were sad, they are too. Owner and animal, when they are very close, take on very similar appearances, as far as the two species can. Look at the owner of a dog, any dog. A thin dog has a slim owner. A fact dog has a fat owner. They seem to have similar features. It is the same thing as people who were married for a long time, they seem to blend, and take over each other's personal traits and behaviour, even to a certain extent their appearance. In old age men and women change. When sex is not the dominant factor any more, they become very similar. Interesting, isn't it?

I am a believer in Life, and Life is for the Living, here and now. There is a good old-fashioned saying "what you can do today, don't put off till tomorrow" and "tomorrow might never come." I am a total believer that today's the day; so don't put things off, live now, and don't say I will do so and so when I retire; when the sun comes out; when it rains; when the children grow up. You don't know God's plan for you, do you? You can't read the Infinite mind with your underdeveloped finite mind. You don't know your own destiny, do you?

That does not mean you cannot know other people's destiny. You can be the world's best Medium/Psychic Clairvoyant or Clairsentient/Clairgustient. This does not mean you will know what is going to happen to you. I believe that is a very good thing.

If you know today what is going to happen to you tomorrow, what would you do? Since you can't do anything about it, accept this as the way of life here. This side of life there is death. After this, when you actually die, there is only freedom and choice again. You're departed loved ones are all waiting for you and life begins anew. You'll never be sick again. You will shine outwardly, all your thoughts can be seen in an Aura (in your energy field) you won't be able to lie in the Spirit World, it would show very quickly. You can't be dishonest, a crook, or a liar, or a cheat – it will show! On the other hand there is no need for it.

The first place you will find yourself will not exactly be Paradise, but the lower astral plane. In that existence things are not much better than here, they are better, but not as good as they could be. You look around and meet your Guides, who will usher you to your loved ones – this is the time to re-unite with them.

You will notice that everybody is young, or as old in appearance as they want to be, and is comfortable for them to be. You can choose too. Do you want to look 20? 30? in appearance? Very few choose to be older. Children have grown up in the Spirit Side and even aborted ones are living and well, stillbirth ones are doing fine. They will greet you since you will not know them – they will have to let you know who they are.

Our Life is an Open Book   But We Write the Pages!

CHAPTER 21

TELEKINESIS, or Moving Objects from a Distance

This needs sheer concentration focusing on the object with all your mind. We can move keys, or a matchstick, on a table, by thought alone. Please start with a matchstick by really focusing on it and saying 'move, move, move'! Hopefully you will succeed! Uri Geller did similar things with metal objects, willing them to bend – bend – bend! We are not trying that. You just want to move a matchstick on the table. Keep concentrating on it – and see it moving (even if it is not doing it yet) and eventually it should take off, move a bit, or a lot!

It is a question of energy – yours – you send out your thoughts very positively – which moves mountains, if, not at least, that matchstick, or paper serviette, or whatever else you are thinking or willing to make move.

Always remember you'll need patience, and it will take a long time – but, if you don't get fed up with it, just stick with it. Whatever you want to make move, will move! If you do this exercise with a group of friends the more the energy the better the result might be. However, it has nothing to do with the Spirit World. It is shared psychic power, mind power, mind-stuff, call it what you like. It is concentrated energy thought – sent out very positively – giving way to powerful forces. One-day you might just move that mountain too, all within reason.

Eventually it will yield to your will, but don't try very heavy things at first. Don't forget the power of suggestion, and the most powerful force is your own mind!

You can harness your mind-ability. I wish you good luck with your trials! Patience and focusing are needed. Concentrate all your mind with all your might to focus on what you want to achieve. Try and try again – it is not easy but it can be done, I assure you! I know!

Our Life is an Open Book   But We Write the Pages!

CHAPTER 22

THE PENDULUM

Well here's a subject for you – the Mighty Pendulum! Pendulum power is divination – using a rod is a different exercise than using the Pendulum. I am able to use it to find over a map dowsing areas, missing people, missing pets or missing articles, whichever is the case, and every case is different! When the pendulum turns to the right it is always say yes. When it turns to the left it means no, and if it just swings back and forth in a diagonal line, no answer is given, but you can give your own interpretation. You can make it your very own tool – it is wonderful in the right hands.

You can go to the beach to look for coins, or beer bottle tops if you're unlucky! Just ask is it here? You can write your questions down, and ask the Pendulum for an answer. You can put your questions to a circle – if they link together in a formation of a no. 8 – then run your Pendulum over each circle back to the middle, and let your pendulum swing, and wait for it to give you the right answer. Try not to influence it while it swings. If the question is for you, it is easier to give an answer to other people (I have found it that way, anyway). You can dowse over photographs with this method. Who is alive? Is he/she living, or not living? I have done that in the James Randi Psychic Investigator TV show, and I only made one mistake!

You can ask it is the place right for me where I live?
Am I going to be successful?

Shall I pass my exams?

Is the name that I was given right for me?

It is a fact that numerology is the science of numbers. Numerology is very ancient, and originally comes from the Arab world. Every number has a meaning. It is not, however, the aim of this book to teach you numerology.

Astrology is the same. You can learn that too. It is not easy, but once you know it, you're probably going to like it too, depending on your enthusiasm.

Our Life is an Open Book   But We Write the Pages!

CHAPTER 23
PENDULUM READING

Many books have been written about the Pendulum. The Pendulum can be a crystal one, extended on a six to eight inch chain, or the one I use is a brass one. It is a Carrier Pendulum. Why? Because you can open it – and place human hair in it for a more accurate reading, or Animal Hair for a missing person, or for a missing Cat or Dog, or any furry animal. If it is a bird, I can place a feather in it too, and dowse over a map to find what I am looking for.

It works! All I need is a good, very detailed map, and somehow that Carrier Pendulum takes me to the spot where the missing person or animal is – or can be found. The pendulum gives me not just places, but answers to time-related questions, by turning right for a Yes answer, and left for a definite No. If it is in between that means there is not a definite answer at the moment.

The pendulum is quite a wonderful tool in the right hands. I have used it many times to give dates and/or times, and out of 100 tries I get 90 % correct! Many times people have phoned me up to tell me how correct it has proved to be.

It is also good for health-related problems. It gives me the correct answer any time. I can hold a Pendulum to an expectant mother's stomach and asked a question – is this a boy? It will turn right. If it is a girl it will turn

The Fledglings Way to Mediumship

left. Mind you there is a problem with twins, but that doesn't happen very often!

1. So we can use it to find Missing Persons.

2. Missing Pets.

3. Finding health problems.

4. In pregnancy, we can predict the sex of the unborn child.

5. We can ask other questions too. Have I got that job?
   Is that job good for me?
   Shall I take that job?

Don't ask silly questions!

Use the Pendulum with Dignity. Use that tool for others only when you're confident about its use. You could find, with the Pendulum, someone's birthday, where the person has come from a country that does not have registered birth facilities. If your house or flat/apartment hunting, you can ask is that the right place for me? If the answer is yes – take it!

You can use it to find Water in Water Divination – crystals buried in the ground and not visible to the human eye.

Cornwall is full of crystals so take your Pendulum with you if you go to that part of England.

Treasure Hunting

Don't forget your old faithful partner, the Pendulum, to be used for this purpose.

Before you go on a car journey you can ask is the traffic going to be a problem, or not? Whatever the case you will get the right answer!

The pendulum is a wonderful tool, so learn to use it wisely!

Get acquainted with your Pendulum, and make it your very own tool.

Don't force the Pendulum to answer your questions – it will on its own accord!

Don't use it all the time. Don't get obsessed with it – I know quite a few people who did! It is not to be used for trivial purposes – but only for good. A peaceful mind is needed in the Alpha State when you ask the question or questions. And you must not ask more than once the same question at any one sitting.

Be patient with yourself.

Be patient with your Pendulum.

Patience will pay dividends.

You will become a better dowser.

And your Pendulum will give 10 out of 10 correct replies!

Don't ask questions like am I going to be rich? They are silly, and not what the pendulum is intended to do. What you can ask is there any negative energy here? You will get the right answer!

If you want to use it for 'Feng Shui' or Space Clearing the Chinese way, ask "shall I put the bed here?" The South-West position is good, but ask your Pendulum anyway, because it depends where you live. West facing is also good for house or flat/apartment hunting. Ask your Pendulum is the west facing place right for me? Would my life changed if I emigrated to Australia? The probable answer to that is Yes. Ask another question. Would Australia be right for me? Shall I move? Why do I really want to move? Ask yourself, and don't bother your Pendulum – it is a trivial question.

You are the maker or breaker of your own life. You should be the Master of your own Destiny, and if you're not, you are tossed on the waves like a sinking ship. There is something seriously wrong, either with you or your inner self, or what your very own self has created for you – your very own Destiny.

Don't forget for a minute, all is Karma – Cause and Effect. You get what you get – because in some point in your life you have become very negative. You can't ask Negative questions from your Pendulum – you will get Negative answers!

Become the Master of yourself and your destiny, and of your Pendulum, which is a good, positive tool in the right hands.

The pendulum is Powerful.

The pendulum is Great.

The Pendulum is only a tool – don't forget that!

The pendulum is designed to help others in need, and not for personal gain – not for Lottery Numbers either, otherwise every Psychic would be a multi-millionaire, which is the furthest thing from the Truth! One cannot help oneself as a Psychic – but only others – those who really need it. Not because greed takes the person over – envy is not the right ingredient, I am afraid. If you have an honest and sincere need we can help you with that – with the Pendulum!

Justice will be done in the end. Just ask "am I sincere in what I'm doing for others?" Watch your Pendulum move! Hopefully it will move Right, which means a Yes. It isn't a divine tool, but a helpful, good, positive one – mainly to help other people. If you've got the highest good in mind, you will use it the Right Way, to help others, and not yourself.

On the other hand, if, for instance, you have forgotten where you left your car keys, you can ask that question – where did my car keys go? Are they on the table? Are they are under the table, the bed, in the car? You will get a truthful reply to that honest, sincere, querying question. That is the difference! You will get the answer you need! Be honest with yourself, and others, and you will always get the right answer to your questions. The Power is within your own self, and not in the pendulum. Remember that! First the pendulum has nothing to do with Mediumship or the Spirit World. This is a Psychic tool. The Medium only needs an open mind and open heart to be able to receive communications from the Spirit Side.

Spirits do not deal in looking for your keys or other such issues. Only the Psychic tool is useful for that.

I suppose I am lucky being a Medium and a Psychic as well. I suppose I have the best of both worlds, you may think, but all I have got is there to serve others. You can try likewise.

"I think (as Descartes said) therefore I am." (Rodin's sculpture 'The Thinker')

I must add "You are what you think!" All is mind stuff. The

extension of the mind/brain are the hands – and the extension of that is the Pendulum. Now you know!

Dowsing Rods

You can make them from a coat hanger. You hold one in one hand and the other in the other hand in the form of a V. You then can find mainly metals, water, petrol, oil, or whatever else you might be looking for. The divining or dowsing rod is especially suited for finding water.

The rods do not have to be made of metal, they can be just two twigs working in the same way on the beach, in the countryside or an open spaces. It is amazing what you can find with patience – and it is great fun too!

Cornwall and Somerset are wonderful places to find old coins, and God only knows what else. Don't keep some things to yourself, they might be National Treasures, and they belong to the British nation, if you find those kind of artefacts. There are plenty of gold coins lying around to be discovered in King Arthur's land, that's a fact. Try Dowsing and see what happens. You will find things, but there is no guarantee what. Good dowsing, and good success!

Our Life is an Open Book   But We Write the Pages!

CHAPTER 24

ARE YOU A PSYCHIC?

Are You – Could You Be a Medium?

Be honest and ask yourself this question. Think about it, and however long it will take you will come up with an answer.

I had a vague idea about this when I was 13 years old. Do you want to wait until a Psychic or a Medium points out to you that you are a Psychic, or a Medium, or even a Healer?

How do you know you are a Psychic? How do you know you're not a Psychic? It's easy!

You meet somebody for the first time and there is an instant rapport or an instant dislike. Score 10 for yes. Score 2 for no.

You enter a building and feel nauseated, sick to your stomach. The feeling is not right, or you don't feel any past emotions here. Every building tells a story. If you can pick up that from the atmosphere (or ether) that is left behind, you have scored 10. If not, 2.

You go for a holiday to Australia. It seems very familiar! Have you been there before (I mean in a previous life or time) and a kind of deja-vu experience strikes you.

If you feel you have visited there before, score 10. You don't feel that, but you feel something. Score 2.

You look into the air, and you see little particles sparkling in the atmosphere. Score 20. You don't see anything, score 0.

You see a ring around the moon in full colour, like a diving belt. The more colour you're able to see, the better it is.
Three colours around the moon score 10.
Two colours around the moon score 5.
One colour around the moon score 2.
No colour at all – can't see any score 0.

To sum up your psychic ability, 50 is a very good high score. A low score is between 8 – 11.

If not good enough try again, until you feel you can see not with your physical eyes but with your third eye. You can learn to do that which will make you a gifted person. You can see pictures in your mind, or outside, whichever way you see it, it is a good and valuable seeing experience for sure.

Our Life is an Open Book   But We Write the Pages!

CHAPTER 25

POTENTIALITY

You have got Mediumship-potential if you have ever heard your name called when no one was there – not to Physical eyes anyway. You are not Schizophrenic – you are what we call very Mediumistic, and almost probably ClairAUDIENT. You will hear Spirits – you do already!

So the Potential is there. When you are ready for further development you will hear much more. The Spirit has to trust you first, and it is slowly opening up to you. First you will be a fledgling, but slowly will learn, as we all had to, to sit for the Spirit, while we sing "Silently now I wait for Thee!" It is wonderful to develop the ability. I would not have had it in any other way. I love God and the Spirit World, and I hope I am a decent instrument for them.

I also heard small tiny bells ringing when I started to develop my abilities. Later on the noise has got louder and LOUDER. No wonder Quasimodo has gone deaf. The Spirits can be very loud, or they can just whisper. It all depends. On the tape it is a tiny whisper, if you're lucky. But when you hear them, some are very clear and others not so. Mind you, they never repeat things! They always seem in no hurry to get their message over, even though they have got all eternity, but they are quite busy on the other side, I know.

Anyway, it is lovely to hear them, or the bells, or whatever else we gather from them.

When messages start to come through from them they are important, very important. After all Spiritualism and Mediumship is built on that – Spirit Communication and our 7 principles, plus the Spiritual Philosophy and OUR way of life.

To Live the Spiritual Life

Have a plain, pure life, don't eat any meat, so a good vegetarian diet is very important, together with drinking plenty of WATER. Mediumship is thirsty work, and most Mediums laugh about that! Mediumship is not doom and gloom, and it can be very funny too – especially when Spirit Persons make jokes! They haven't lost their sense of humour, it might have got even more intense. It seems to me that there is plenty to laugh about in the Spirit Side of Life. They are free of pain and happy. All are well, extremely happy, loved, and reaching out to share their own bigger joy with you too!

Life can be joyous here and now too. It is up to you how you see things, either you can cry or you can laugh – your own attitude towards all these things counts a lot, even in development. A positive outlook on life works wonders, especially in development. You attract the good, better things to you, and nicer people too from the Spirit Side of Life!

"Like attracts like!" here, now, and definitely from beyond the veil. Death is rebirth to better things yet to come.

Death is the doorway to the Spirit World, to love and light eternal, and you become the ambassador for the Spirits, but you will have to work on yourself a lot to be a good Instrument. It sounds like hard work. It is, but it is worth every bit of suffering to achieve your goal – to be a perfected, if not totally perfect instrument to the Spirit World!

It is much nicer in the higher regions of the World of the Spirit. The lower astral Spirit speaks for itself. The higher Spirit is on Higher Vibratory rate, which is much, much nicer.

Some Spirit people coming from that place are mainly our Spirit Helpers, Spirit Guides, door-keepers, but not relatives. If they have progressed that far they do not return any more. We must also not hold them back on their journey, by grieving for them.

They are 'Alive' and very well, but they find it extremely difficult to make their return to here. This is a very low place, this Earth plane of ours. It is very dense and they find it very difficult, if they have progressed so far, to lower their vibrations to ours. Hence they don't communicate with us any more. They still love you, and they love us, but they have their new life, and you have yours – till we meet up again. You know how it is here, after the rain, and the sun shines – we see a rainbow! When we cross over, and see that white bridge with the rainbow hanging over it, we know we have crossed over – because of the out-shining love on the other side of that white rainbow bridge. Your pet will run towards you, if you had one. Friends, family all greet you, and help is also available for progression to the higher side.

You will need a lot of confidence at first as a student Medium Fledgling – but you will soon learn to differentiate between vibrations, descriptions of Spirit People. They will test you, and your patience too, not giving you their names. You will learn they will only do it if you ask them for it. It is a question of total co-operation between the Guide Spirit person and a Medium. Harmony is needed. Harmonise, put aside your ego, and intellect. 'Let the Spirit work, not me', should be your key phrase.

Aim not to use your ego, not to think of gain, but to feel love for all, and with dedication and humility, integrate your personality, utilising the higher you – your Higher Self must reach out to all that is good.

Always aim higher, and all the doors will open for you to walk with God and your Guides, and here, feel or see Spirits; so you can, metaphorically, have a foot here, and the other over there. Make sure you are well-adjusted, and are not malnourished – you will need all your energy.

Mediums become well padded, and are definitely built for comfort, not for speed. We all put on weight. It is supposed to give us some greater protection. You will find that plenty of fat will be distributed around your solar plexus. But it is important you feel all feelings there, before you take them up higher to the throat chakra (one of the energy centres, you remember) then to the crown of the head, when all things open up, and higher communications are achieved.

The Chakras or Energy Centres Explained

The lowest Chakra is the base Chakra. Its colour is Red. It is located at the base of the spine.

The second is the Sacral or Solar Plexus Chakra. It is around the navel area, and its associated colour is orange.

The third is the spleen Chakra. Its colour is yellow. It is hard to explain exactly near where it is located.

The fourth is the heart Chakra. Its colour is green. It is located in the middle of the breastbone.

The fifth is the throat Chakra. Its colour is blue. It is located at the hollow of the throat.

The sixth is the Third Eye Chakra (so I call it a Brow Chakra). Its colour is purple or indigo. Its location is in the middle of the forehead – which is exactly in the Pituitary Gland area.

The seventh is the Crown Chakra. Its colour is violet or white. It is located at the Top or Crown of the Head.

Working Practices

Whatever you do, please work with the greatest possible integrity. People will trust you because you're a Medium, Psychic, or whatever. Never let people down, you have to try to give your best at all times, which is not as easy as it sounds. It is a hard job to be a good and trustworthy Medium, and don't forget you're only as good as your last reading. People will judge you by what you are able to give them. If they are very eager to hear from a particular person only, they create a block, and if they have told you the person who they want to get in touch with, they make it nearly impossible for you to operate properly.

In cases like that you have to give all the information you have gathered, and about people you have not been told about. Usually I would love to put a padlock on some sitter's mouths, to allow them to open them only when it is necessary to say a simple yes or no. You do not need any information from them. If you are gratuitously given it, it hampers you rather than helps you a great deal! No honest Medium ever needs any lead. We don't need to be helped, after all the communication comes from the Spirit

World, and the less we know, before we hear from the Spirit, the better the communication will be. I can watch out for this. I know what it does for me, for instance. The Spirit would have told me anyway, and I would rather hear it from them. I do not need any information myself from the sitter. So when you go to see a Medium, try to remember that. I can vouch for that – no information from you is needed.

You come to find information, not to give it to the medium. It is not conducive, and it is not positive. We do not need any information from you. We need peace and harmony. When you start with a prayer for instance, you will get the link with the Spirit World. If you were a trained Medium it means we open the door to the Spirit World. Open it, and close it once it is over.

Always close down before you go back to your everyday life after the consultation or sitting, and go and have a coffee or a tea, but definitely plenty of water. Then go for a walk, exercising your body after the mind has been fully engaged.

Everything must be done in moderation. As a Medium you cannot burn the candle at both ends. You definitely need vitamins – you will recall I have written earlier about food and how important that it is to eat well, and wisely. The brain vitamins B6 and B12 and C are essential for your mind, and E and Beta Carotene are quite helpful too.

You should look after yourself if you are a Medium or Healer, and try not to give your own energy. Mind you, some of it will be used, and that is why you will have to have vitamin supplements. You must also eat all the fruits of the season. Gentle exercise helps too, such a stretching and reaching up towards the stars.

Our Life is an Open Book   But We Write the Pages!

CHAPTER 26

THE GRIEVING PROCESS

Some people need counselling when a loved one dies. Others, if they know mediums exist, turn to us for relieving the pain, or the agony of guilt, which most people are bound to feel. Why didn't I help more? Why is he/she gone? Am I being punished? I am sorry to say you're feeling alone, and you are grieving for yourself. Suddenly the world is a very hostile and a very unfriendly place when you find yourself in that position. You can use your 'Alone-ness' to learn to expand or to have a break-down, see someone to talk to about your feelings. Other bereaved persons do not want to talk at all. These feelings once turned inside you, can suffocate you. You need to air your feelings whichever way you can! Find your way through life's jungle, and, eventually feel contented, even at a later date.

Usually your parents die before you – it is the normal order of things. Whoever goes first you have to face the facts. No more goodbyes, no hellos, only when you are re-united. For good on the Spirit Side. Until then you can hear from them. Seek help – it is available. The grieving process can go on for quite some time if you don't get help. It varies with individuals, usually three to five years, then it gets easier. If you have seen a Medium who was able to re-unite you with your relatives or friends, you know life has not ended here. It goes on, so you grieve less, and the pain heals in time. Everyone has got their own time-scale. First of all you seek that most important communication, then comes acceptance, finally.

We don't just accept the situation as it is not so final, not so sad, and not so bad. If you seek enlightenment, or if you're lucky enough to communicate with your loved ones, it is healing. Healing takes place when you talk to somebody about it. If you seek the Light you will find inner peace. You will find inner peace, and that most wanted survival evidence and the Light ahead. There is always light at the end of the tunnel. And after the dark despair, the sun will come out once again, to shine on you too.

If you can turn to God, and want to develop your abilities after severe blows, obviously it is the right time for you to seek that ever-shining light, so you will find peace in your life, and you can help many others, who are just as much in the dark as you were.

Peace will be your guide and helper – inner Peace in the great knowledge that your loved ones are only a thought away, and when you need them they are there to come to your aid. You will not be aware of that, but if you send your love and loving thoughts to them every day, the link will never be broken, and it will keep afresh. They will be with you when they can be. They will come and visit you. They can come in your dream state. You will see them clearly and hear them too, but not all of you can. Remember you're not yet a Medium, but at last, for once in your life, you will have had a psychic or spiritual experience of some kind. Don't dismiss it as something you've only imagined which did not really happen. It does and it will – leave that door open.

Sometimes when you are in need, or for whatever other reason, they do come. Don't forget the grave is empty, they are not there, and your Spirit-Soul Self never ever dies for the Life of you.

They do pay visitations. They do care about your welfare, and your state of mind. They love you just as much as when they were here, or even more so! It is only a very temporary separation, and life here is, however long here, still relatively short, in comparison with all ETERNITY over there.

Our Life is an Open Book   But We Write the Pages!

CHAPTER 27

REINCARNATION

Some people believe we can return, and have been here before, even in, say, Atlantis, before the Atlantians went to Egypt. There are many lives and many survival stories – as in the book written by Roger Wolger, an American Author, who wrote "MANY LIVES, MANY SELVES." You need a good Past-life Regressionist, like Petrene Soames, in Houston, Texas, U.S.A. She took people back to the various lives they lived here before, on a television show, which lasted three and half hours! I don't deal with that sort of thing, but I thought I should mention it.

She can also take you to your Future, and your own Death, so you won't be afraid when it comes to you. Ron Moody has written many books on past lives. It is a nice thought. Speaking personally, I don't want to come back here.

Some people believe in "karma" cause and effect. I do too, but I believe free will exists, and you can choose if you ever want to make your return here or not. There are many other physical planes like Earth in the Universe.

We wait and see – it will be shown to us in the higher life, what kind of humans are living there, and it would be up to you to see if you would like to be part of that.

Some are more evolved than others, which is just like here. Some humans here, I would say most, are very primitive, compared to other civilisations, even in the Earth's long past. Every civilisation brought something very special into being, until, perhaps, we lost all trace of it.

History is an interesting subject. Looking at life objectively, you have plenty enough to learn here and now, and more in the higher life. The learning process has to go on. That is the secret of this Life, and of many on the other side too. The rest of it is hidden, we are not ready here to know about it.

Our Life is an Open Book   But We Write the Pages!

CHAPTER 28

REALISATION – THE OTHER SIDE

When you crossover Realisation will draw you on, you will slowly begin to look around, and, after the sleep-state, you will be reborn again; will feel full of energy, and ready to go. You were not in a limbo state, your faculties are back in full swing. You are young again, and full of energy.

The other side is wonderful, it is full of light and wonder. You will have houses to live in, something you always wanted, perhaps, this side, but were never able to achieve – you will get that over there.

You will slowly become aware and awakened to all sorts of possibilities, and new responsibilities. You will realise you are fully ALIVE, more than ever before, and happy! You will feel no physical pain of any kind – it is all left behind you with your physical body. You will realise your full faculties and you can use all your six senses.

You will be aware in every sense more than ever before, and ready to go for it, for whatever life has got to offer you in the higher existence of Life. I call it Awakening! You will enjoy your new life!

CHAPTER 29

BACK TO EARTH – HAUNTINGS

Many buildings are haunted, old buildings and old inns especially. It is the earthbound entities, who do not want to move on, who are making a big nuisance of him or herself. Many times objects are moved around, not always in a noisy way, but they can be. Every entity operates differently. The suicides are still here, and getting progressively very angry. They cannot be seen, but they can be heard!

Some others can't understand why other people can't see them! It is pitiful when I enter this kind of atmosphere. I am able, more often than not, to pick up on that entity, and talk to it. One thing they cannot stand is to be ignored, hence the reason they are creating the disturbances. It makes them happier to be taken notice of! Any notice they feel they are given is better than to feel completely ignored! England is famous for its haunted castles, and the Tower of London is very haunted.

You have only to think about Henry VIII and his seven wives – the block – heads rolling – two wives still around – and looking for their lost heads! Queen Anne Boleyn is often seen, not only by Mediums, but ordinary visitors.

It is a strange place, the Tower, with its RAVENS.

Think about Edgar Allan Poe, the famous poet who said

"said the Raven
Never more."

Strange noises can be heard, and airy footsteps, especially at night in the Tower of London.

The other fairly haunted place is the famous London Dungeon – chains rattling – whispers – winds for no reason – and after all, what is in there – a few wax figures – but there seems to be much more than that, besides the wax figurines. Perhaps the owners of the wax bodies come and have a look at themselves?

Many books have been written on famous haunted buildings in Britain. I would ask the reader to delve into them, as I only wished to introduce a few examples in the preceding lines by way of introduction to these strange and sometimes tortured entities. You are not going to run out and look for lost souls just now, you should leave that to the experts, mediums who specialise in Spirit Rescue.

CHAPTER 30

RESCUE – CIRCLES

In rescue circles a Medium and like-minded people might stay behind, and gather to offer up a prayer opening to lost souls who should be in the world of the Spirit, but somehow got lost, and never got there. If this gathering sits with all sincerity, someone will knock on the door – a lost Spirit! It can be quite traumatic – there will be a lot of explaining to do to the Spirit person to go to the light – perhaps following my Guide, or whatever else is the case.

I have sat in that kind of a circle. I must emphasise it does not suit everyone. Not everybody wants to deal with quite difficult Spirits. For instance I had a young men who died in a motorcycle accident. His name was John, and he came in very distressed. He said he was only here because he has seen the light – and I had tears rolling down my cheeks. In the end he left with my Guide.

That was one more successful rescue!

Some just hang around, and do not want to move on. One day they will, when it dawns on them that they do not belong here any more. This is when we say goodbye to them, and upstairs they say hello, or welcome.

It is terrible to hang around here without the physical body, and no one can see you or hear you – it is a real Hell on Earth!

CHAPTER 31

HOPE, CHARITY, KARMA

Development

Whatever you do Hope should be on your side, whatever else you give up on!

Never ever give up on hope! Yours especially! Only with a positive and balanced mind – never mind the lifestyle – can you ever hope to develop your abilities as a Medium.

Hope should be your friend, your Mentor. Never give up on yourself, and never give up on the Spirit World. The Spirits will come to your aid only when they see fit to do so, or you were fit for it. Life is Lesson-Learning. Like it or not, that is what it is all about. Think about it. If you have Riches they can be taken away, and, at the end, your coffin is empty. You came naked into the world, and take nothing away with you, except what you have learnt here. So from the soul point of view, suffering is good for you. You can't learn anything if everything has always gone well in your life! Be glad if it has not!

Tests

Tests or difficulties are important. You can't learn them in an easy way. You must learn the hard way! Envy no one – what for? That very wealthy person might die of cancer, or even better, younger age. You don't need millions to be happy, or even semi-contented.

Life will, possibly, give you a few blows, but you must be strong to withstand it. It should make you stronger. Try not to be weak. Strength is a virtue. Learn to be able to stand on your own two feet at all times! Help others! Help the helpless animals, because they need you. Helpless people need you too – the weaker needs the stronger – so cultivate strength. Just say "I am strong and I will remain strong! No wind or storm can move me. I stand firm. I make a difference, even in a humble way."

Without hope you might as well not exist! Without hope you will despair! Faith keeps you going, so any faith is good. Believe in yourself and God!

Our Life is an Open Book   But We Write the Pages!

CHAPTER 32

CHARITY

Giving. Some people don't even like the sound of the word. They don't understand the law of cause and effect, or Karma.

Giving is Receiving!

When you give it frees you. It should make you happy that you can. Always remember charity is the key. If you can't give money, give what you can. Yourself. Visit hospitals. Help others. There are millions of ways to do it. Someone somewhere needs you, too. The old, the lonely, the one in pain. It can be mental or physical help. You can lend a helping hand. It is good for your advancement in the Spiritual ether too.

Giving from the heart is the best way to give truly and honestly. Gently does it! Don't make a song and dance about it if you help others. Keep quiet about it. Go quietly about your daily business and blessings will come to you!

CHAPTER 33

DEVELOPMENT

So this is your development. It is not enough to sit in a circle once a week, for an hour or so. Meditation is also a daily routine or practice. Practice makes perfect.

Surround yourself with beautiful crystals. Have a wind chimer, and an indoor waterfall, and try to live the Spiritual Life, in preparation for your forthcoming Psychic and Spiritual work.

Once I heard a Medium from the platform announcing "I don't like pigeons!" What a statement to make! God has created all I love, including pigeons. I like all life forms. So should you too! It is very sad if you do not. I am very wary of people who do not like dogs or even cats. What is wrong with them? Surely they must hate people too!

Development I

It means putting your dislikes aside, and trying to make a better human being of yourself.

Development II

To reach to the Higher Forces, and Higher frequency of Communication. My Guides work with me in an extremely fast way. All the information flows – but it can vary, possibly, with other mediums. Their Guides might work in a lower, or slower vibratory rate.

In this development you will learn how to attune with your Helpers/Doorkeepers/Mentors, or so-called Spiritual Guides. They will appear to you however vaguely – from time to time, and they will talk to you. They can be audible, or just in your own mind. You will learn to realise when they are contacting you, and when they are around you. You can say a prayer to help to ask for your Guide to attend, and to help you with the Communication (at a later stage of Development). At first there is only attainment, and breathing. It is important to count your breaths. Try to leave the World behind for that short time you sit for the Spirit. Let there be Peace and Love in your heart. Leave all your daily worries behind you when you enter the development classroom. It is not very conducive if you worry, for instance, what you will cook when you get home, how will your job go! Have perfect Faith in your Helpers, sit in a peaceful and positive mood. It will also help others in the same circle – or class – to progress.

Some of you will progress fairly rapidly, others will take a few years longer. The ones who progress faster than any one else is or are born mediums. Mediums are really born, and not made! Remember that. However, you can give it a try. Hopefully you will get something out of it, even so, you will never be a fully-fledged medium, but with the greatest of patience (few know the meaning of that) you will get somewhere. The Spirit has to trust you first of all, and can only give you as much at a time as you will be able to understand. Some leave the circle, and go elsewhere. They did not fit in, or they didn't progress, or for whatever other reason. Sometimes the change is for the better, but not always.

Don't forget you have to like the people you sit with, if not love them, but you must find the place, and people in a peaceful and conductive positively energised atmosphere. Otherwise run – if there is not a supercharged atmosphere present. You won't get great expectations from every meeting, so get out of it. It might not be right for whatever reason to carry on, if that is the case. You feel you're not getting anywhere there, and, therefore, not happy at all.

Sometimes the Medium who is conducting the circle has got a pet student. You would be better off elsewhere, or sitting at home alone, at the same time every day, for half an hour or so. It is enough. Mind you, it is harder to develop alone, and invite your Guide/Guides to you, so you can sit in safety at home.

Ask for the Gold and White Light to be around you in the circle of White Light and Gold, and to be centred.

Keep your feet on the floor. Sit on a hardback chair, not too comfortably (otherwise you might go to sleep). You're here to work. Close your eyes, and off you go! Play some Healing or New-Age music in the background, if not, a white voice, or white sound is good. A water fountain is the best. It clears the atmosphere. Make sure you have some sea salt nearby in a bowl, for clearance and purity, and, more importantly, for Protection..

You don't know who is coming when you open the door – do you? After all you have invited them. Like attracts like. You've got nothing to be afraid of. Only those similar to you will be attracted to you from the Spirit Side. That is as it should be. If someone else slips through the net and gets through, who you don't want, send them back! You only want the nice people from the Spirit Side – that is so very important. Development is also important. Impatience will lead you astray. Delusion is not a good thing, when the Real One is available for you too.

Patience pays big dividends. Proper training and proper development open the door to wonders, and pure, wonderful messages get through!

It is worth your while not to hurry things. Make sure you are ready. I say again "when the pupil is ready, the master appears! You don't want some mischievous spirits to get through to you, do you?" The pranksters are not funny. But, with patience, the real Spirit Personalities make their presence felt.

Only once in my life did I get very frightened when I saw a Black Mass appearing in a very bizarre shape. It was hard to put it into words. It was beastly and non-human! I shouted at it "Go away, in the name of Jesus! I don't want to see you! Get out!" And as quickly as it had appeared, it disappeared! I would never like to see that ever again! No thank you!

Once-in-a-lifetime is more than enough to see something like that! I asked for my Guides quickly, and the White Light protection, so it will never come to me again! We always have to ask for the White Light protection when we do any Spiritual work. The Dark Forces are watching too, I believe. Don't be vulnerable! Be firm! The firmer you stand, believe me, you make your stand heard a million, billion miles away! They know they can't mess with you! You are working for the Highest. So no low entity can come near you, and if they try, they are the ones who will be running away, and not you!

Don't mess around with any Ouija board! It is not a sensible thing to do. You don't know what will happen, or who you were inviting in! Would you leave your front door open at night? No, you wouldn't! Not even the back door! So no Ouija boards!! That way you invite in the very lowest of entities – and they will not move on! That kind love to stay in the Earth's Atmosphere. They are the abuser types. They could have been murderers, rapists, drug addicts, the lonely, the spiritually bankrupt, alcoholics and the like. So don't leave your door open to them. Otherwise you will have to pay the price!

I don't want to frighten you – but that is the Truth!

There is no quick way to Heaven! There is no fast way to Mediumship either, which is the Highest form of Mediumship and Psychic ability – Communication with the Ministry of Angels and Spirits. Don't try to side-step the important rules. You will pay the price for it, otherwise. You will never get it right! Your life will be a mess! You will be a mess! And so-called Communication will, if anything, only come from the lowest of Astral planes.

Ask for the High Guides. Don't mess with low entities – and you will be on the way to the real thing.

Patience pays dividends, always!

Ask for the Light! So then the Light will never leave you, neither here, neither when you yourself pass on to the Higher Life. Let God be your number one Guide. Then your Guide, then your Higher Self. Perfect the Instrument that is yourself. "To thine own self be true!"

Work on your character. Try to be honest and truthful at all times. Even so, your head will feel it is on the block! So what! You are telling the truth aren't you? So what are you afraid of?

Our Pioneers have suffered. Helen Duncan has been imprisoned under the Witchcraft Act in England, not so very long ago. Now things have improved somewhat. But you can still get persecuted – don't forget that!

You have to be very responsible in whatever you say to people, and if you cannot be, don't be a Medium, or even a Healer! You must understand how to conduct yourself properly at all times. You will meet so many people of so many different backgrounds, you must know how to handle them, and how to conduct yourself especially.

It is not easy to meet all kinds of people, but very rewarding in Spiritual ways. Some will thank you, others will forget you – some will never forget you! Some will return, others recommend you to many more. Some say nothing at all. It does not mean they have not been moved. It is all part of human nature for you. It is worth your while to take up some psychological studies of human behaviour. It will help you a lot in your chosen field – to be a Medium or a Healer/Medium. We know there is more to life than meets the eye, and, yes "Out of the rainbow where Bluebirds fly."

In God's wonderful real paradise in the Higher life, all comes to life again. And that knowledge should not be imparted that easily – but only to a few. You have a chosen a Spirit. Fine! Has a Spirit chosen you? Well that is different!

You have felt it when a child. Someone is close to you, or is talking to you? It was your Guide since birth. But as you grow your Guides will change – because you seek them out, because you feel you have to. You have a Mission in this Life – since I was 13 years of age I knew I am here for a reason. I have been proved right. Some Mediums become very famous, some dedicated ones never seek the limelight, just work quietly for Spirit-serving churches, or helping Animal Welfare. My good friend, the lovely Marion Denny, God bless her, at the age of 79, she serves churches faraway and travels by public transport, and gives all her hard earned money to Animal Charities! There are many like her

– silent, good, solid workers for the Spirit. Silently going around to help as many as they possibly can. It is not an easy life, but a very rewarding one. We pay the price for it too! People are taken away from us. You are left alone to be able to help more, to reach out further. Once we understand that, we won't get angry any more! We can withstand life's blows with great dignity. We know we have made our stand, and Life is for the Living, here and now, and to all Eternity!

As we say "you can't die for the life of you!" We go on forever, and beyond the clouds, in our hidden home, where we are originated from, and where we all return to, our Spiritual Home, to be reunited with all our loved ones, for all ETERNITY – and ETERNITY is a long time!

Some of you probably want to be Guides, some others at a later date. Some of you will be just happy to do the things you never had time to do here. You can write, or paint, or sing, developing your abilities in the Spirit Side. The hidden you will come out to welcome a new day, and new life in what we call Paradise.

Our Life is an Open Book   **But We Write the Pages!**

CHAPTER 34

QUESTIONS OFTEN ASKED OF MEDIUMS

What is it like on the other side? It is brilliant, all splendour in most regions, depending where you find yourself.

How do Spirit people live? Almost in the same way as here, except there is no Carnal Knowledge, you are not in the physical body.

Are Animals there too? Yes, Animals are there too. You can have your own pet with you, who you loved here! Wild animals go to a different plane of existence. They stay wild in the animal kingdom. It would not be fair to them, otherwise.

The important thing is Love, which unites us all forever. It is the strongest bond in the world in ours, and Upstairs it is Love, and a Love alone that unites. Deep, unbroken Spiritual love, sincere and honest deep love, unconditionally it unites us all who are capable of loving to that degree for ever.

I call the here and now the physical phase of life. In that physical phase you have to learn all the tricks of the trade. How to survive, how to be a special human being, or just an ordinary one. But all people are mostly wonderful and magical, because there is only one of you in this world, whoever you are! And you can't replace any one ever! Therefore help people validate their existence. They will thank you for it, if you notice them. You can lift people's spirits by encouragement, and by giving them real help, or mental upliftment, or just give them that special something, so they will believe in themselves, and love you for it. Help them to discover who they really are! Truly wonderful beings. O.K., their AURA here is not so out-shining, and they all have burdens to carry, but however slightly we can lift that burden, and make them laugh and cry at the same time. That is the Medium's real job, not just passing on messages, but always remembering to uplift that person. They need you! Never let anyone walk away from you without trying to put a smile back on their face, after the flood of tears. Bless them and let them go on their way!

No one will teach you ethical handling of people. You must know how to be kind, and have feeling towards everyone you meet. Passionately love God and Spirits. That will lead you to love your fellow human beings too! Most Mediums are good solid human beings, who feel very deeply. Compassion should be your motto always!

The most important word in your vocabulary should be compassion! And if you end up on a desert island take that word with you anyway. In my book of human behaviour first and foremost comes compassion — towards all beings! I emphasise all beings, not just humans. Animals are just as important to me.

Animals are your friends and mine, and they are our younger brethren. Don't you ever forget that!

Our Life is an Open Book   But We Write the Pages!

CHAPTER 35

TWO SIDES TO ALL THINGS

Where there is God there is evil.

Where there is black there is white.

When you enter certain environments like hospitals, there is usually a very heavy atmosphere.

When I came out of an operation, quite a long one, and I felt I was coming round, being placed back in my bed, and the hospital curtains drawn, I never saw so many spirit entities in my life as I saw then. They just appeared from nowhere. Were they people who had died there, and had just come to seem me? Were they interested in me, or just curious, or just came to help? Who knows? The interesting thing was that no one I had known or loved came to be there for whatever reason. I thanked them for coming, anyway.

There are always two sides to every coin. There is the light side and the dark side. Thank God I don't often come across the dark side. I feel well protected and usually they do not bother me. The dark side comes sometimes as a Psychic attack. But that is for another chapter.

Our Life is an Open Book **But We Write the Pages!**

CHAPTER 36

PSYCHIC ATTACK

Psychic Protection

When you feel low, that is when they strike – when you feel let down by all unworthy or better things in life, feeling a headache, feeling unlucky, this is the time to send a Psychic attack to you. Not only Psychics can get at you, a negative thought can be sent to you to hit you, making you ill. That is a Psychic attack from the Dark Side.

Whenever you feel it, try and send it back to the sender. You don't wish them any harm, but, whatever they've sent to you, return it like a boomerang. Usually that works very well. Don't forget to ask immediately for God's White Light Protection.

"Dear God help me to see your light, surround my soul, body and mind with the White Light coming from you. Take away all the dark forces that are not meant for me. Seal it with a Gold Light around me, and be my Guide and Helper! Please help me as always! Thank you for sending my Guide to my side now."

CHAPTER 37

AFFIRMATIONS

1. Every Day is a new day, and it may be the best of my life.
2. Without hope there is no life. With hope I go on, my heart is sealed.
3. Love is the essence I freely give to others.
4. I love Life and Life likes me.
5. Nature is renewed every season, and so am I. Every day I can start a new life – I will turn over a new page.
6. I like challenges, and the biggest challenge so far in my life is my life.
7. I am brave. I live!
8. The world belongs to those who are willing to put something back into it
9. Bravery is to go on, despite adversity.
10. Smile – it might not happen!
11. Nothing is as good or bad as you think!
12. All things are there to serve a purpose.
13. Life is for the Living!
14. I never give up improving myself!
15. I don't expect – I give first!
16. I greet every day as a new challenge yet to come for being alive!
17. Smiles say more than any words can!
18. A smile is International. I don't have to speak another language for that.
19. Cheerfulness brings Positive Results.

20. My outlook on Life is Positive. I am an achiever.
21. I don't pull wool over anyone's eyes, and I don't expect any one to do the same to me either.
22. I am alert to new opportunities, and they won't pass me by.
23. I am Alive! I am Psychic!
24. I can feel the raindrops. I can see the golden molecules dancing in the air in the golden sunlight. I am vibrant. I am energetic!
25. Don't miss the moment – it might never come again!
26. One day at a time, but I make the best of every passing moment.
27. On my grave it will read

> "She has lived on earth
> She helped.
> Duty done!"

28. Don't expect the apples from the trees to fall in your mouth.
29. Expect everything and expect nothing. Don't try too hard – just hard enough. To know when is enough that would make you a Genius!
30. Strive to be happy, and if not, accept your lot.
31. With acceptance a lot of things get better.
32. Heal your thoughts before you think. Heal your body before illness falls on you. Think positively so you can enjoy life a bit more.
33. The simplest things are the best, and the cheapest. Hot sunshine, green grass and a smile.
34. Give first, always.
35. Don't ask for favours. Your creator knows your needs.
36. All you need is Wisdom. Wisdom makes you Free.
37. For inspiration, I would take Wagner to a desert island with me.
38. Nothing is as bad as your own thoughts at night.
39. The night-time is a bad adviser.
40. Think while the sun is shining.

41. Be brave – nobody else can do it for you!
42. Your thoughts count. Watch them.
43. If you're not happy in your environment, create the one you want – first in thought – then it will come to you.
44. I learn to communicate, validate and appreciate others. I value myself, so I value others too.
45. Everything begins with oneself to make improvements – change your thoughts. Don't play the part of a victim – you become one if your own thoughts will trap you into it. Don't entertain it!
46. I am a being of Love and Light. I am worthy of Love. I do love myself, if not, I don't love others either.
47. I am a capable being.
48. I appreciate good people. I show them love and give them little pearls of wisdom. I don't ever expect any return of any good deed.
49. I appreciate God's lovely garden in this world. The people in it are the only problem.
50. We can't change others. Try to change yourself not to suit others, but to suit you. That is a big difference, and once you understand that you can really go for it!
51. Old Sages have plenty of Wisdom. We have to create new ones, with new ideals to live by.
52. Life can be a stage – but you have to learn how to play your part in the Cosmos.
53. The World is shrinking – as you grow older your body expands, and gets larger. Life is a funny thing – you might as well laugh.
54. Think about good things – only you will bring it about.
55. A smile a day surely keeps any doctor away!
56. Life is a basket, but don't put all your eggs in it. Think about that one! God gave you brains and abilities – learn to use them.
57. Life is to say I have no regrets.

58. Love is to say Forever!
59. Mountains can be molehills if I wish them to be.
60. I minimise things. I thus simplify my life.
61. Nothing is larger than Life – except the Eternal.
62. Those who have given you life can give you peace of mind too – if you were to ask for it.
63. Since we all live on borrowed Time, smile more often. It is healthy – so we die happier.
64. Inner peace has to be earned and worked on. It does not come easily.
65. Since life is everlasting why worry about minute details? Things last longer than you!
66. Thought forms can affect your physical life. Create good ones, not only for your own benefit, but for others. The world is full of Negative thought forms created by others. It can make one sick.
67. Send a blessing out every day – if not to any one person, but to the world. It needs Healing! It needs prayer. It needs good thoughts.
68. Send Love and Light to all corners of the Universe, to make of this World a more ideal place to live in. It seems the inhabitants are rather lethargic.
69. Keep your chin up at all times.
70. Sadness creates more sadness. Negative attracts more negativity. Say enough is enough – I want Love, Light and all the good Positive things in my life. I want success and happiness. You will see the changes. You have asked for them!

So let it be! Hopefully you can learn a few things from this book – a hint, or just one thought even, which helps your on your way. Let it be Mediumship or Psychic-Faculty, or it helps you to live a better Life, then I have done my job well!

It is so very important to me to feel I am helping you, dear reader, even if you come across this book by chance one day. Perhaps you will be that person that will decide bingo! Eureka! I discovered I wanted to be a Medium, or I am a Psychic anyway, let's go for it! I have thus done my job well! If you seek help of any kind the Spirits know your need – you will find the way!

The way is not easy, and the journey is arduous and long, but it is worth every effort!

Some of us are born to be Mediums, others learn to be – whichever is the case. I wish you a speedy Journey, and love and enlightenment when you get weary or sad. Don't ever forget, if we knock, doors are opened, and if we try, we will succeed. At the end of every Tunnel there is the Light!

That everlasting God-light will show you the way – your way, dear reader, to be yourself, or to be what you're capable of being. We can fly in the sleep state, and in the mind nothing is as fast as thoughts.

Spirit Communication shows you that "the fastest way to travel is with the mind – those who know that have wings!" (a quote from the Hopi Indians). Petrene Soames quoted that in her book "The Essence of Self-Healing". Yes – Physician heal thyself! That book is worth a read.

Seek out books – live and learn – you are here for that reason alone!

If God would have given you wings there would be a traffic jam in the sky! Well this world is so chaotic you must find yourself and your own inner deep Peace. You can be even happier trying harder. Mediums and Psychics are usually well adjusted, well balanced people. We have to be – to a show you the way, and it is a requirement from the Spirits. All of us are required to have a healthy mind, body and spirit for the integrated and intricate work I call Psychic Ability and Mediumship.

I wish each and every one of you the best of luck in your life in which you will create your own "Karma", by living the best life you can visualise for yourself. Don't forget that if you don't achieve much here, perhaps it is not meant to be. And the Future you create for yourself today by the way you live now. Spiritualism is a way of life, and I would not change what I know about it for anything!

Earthly values are a very small pittance comparatively with Spiritual ones. And only the Spiritual ones really count a lot in reality. You can't put them on a scale – you can't measure them because it is from a spirit weightless substance – less in this World only – but it counts a lot.

It is a way of life, as Arthur Findlay pointed out in his book " The Way of Life", and in the "Rock of Truth".

Truth is Truth, and that is what we are standing for to pass on the message to you, and all who have their hearts and ears open to want to hear, and are ready for it. Life is Eternal, and nothing is Higher than Truth! When you start searching for your very own truth, I am certain you will find what will make you stronger to withstand all blows, and smile in the knowledge you have come a long way. But that battle is won by you alone! Seek that knowledge – it will give you that freedom now – and the truth makes you free!

The choice is yours, as always. Live like a slave, or dare to seek and Win! I believe the freedom of choice lies with the individual. Choose well, so you can be happy, and discover the real you and your real Destiny!

Our Life is an Open Book But We Write the Pages!

CHAPTER 38

TO LIVE BY THE BOOK

Life continues on the other side, and, as long as you know that, obviously it makes sense to try to live the Spiritual Life. What do I mean by Spiritual? Try to always help others, even if you do not get any thanks for it. And that is very much human nature.

In that case you might be very pleasantly surprised if you never expect much in return for your good deeds. You should know, dear reader, that all things are possible if you believe in that strongly! Not with your mind, but mainly with your heart.

So when you visit hospitals patients may be unreasonable – make allowances – they are sick. It especially applies to any cancer patients.

Their present outlook on life completely changes their concepts of what is life all about, or has been. Their eyes are open to things which otherwise would have stayed hidden. I have seen a few like that. They can be quite unreasonable, or even irrational. But, as I have already mentioned, one has to make allowances. Their suffering is truly horrendous! Try to be gentle with them, if you are a Healer, a good listener, a friend, and a real Councillor, but above all, be very kind! They do not need your pity, but they do need you! They need to open their heart to someone whom they do trust and like. Be a good listener, and heal their pain. Be positive they do need your positivity and hope. Do not talk much about yourself – only if they are interested in your problems – they have more than enough problems themselves. It is better to help them any way you can. Spiritual Healing heals all. Body, Mind, and Spirit – all of them. It is like "Alias" responding to true unconditional love. A Healer is not a Saint. A Healer is only human, but with little knowledge and help from the Spirit World, you can go and Heal and feel good about it!

I have seen many patients with cancer, even inoperable ones. When I feel I can do no more for them I send them back to their doctor. God is a better Healer, and doctors on the other side work with us.

A problem that can arise is that not everyone will ask you to be healed. A golden rule is not to offer to help get the patient better if he/she has not asked you specifically. Leave it to them to ask you! I never offer Mediumship or Healing – only when I had have been asked to do so. If someone intervenes for another person, I can send Distant Healing, which can be just as effective as if you do Contact Healing. In cases of cancer, I have found Contact Healing has worked much better!

I can tell a dog to lie down to receive healing. I will help them – they know! Humans are a problem, sometimes. I love animals. It is so easy to get on with them. Then again, we are surrounded by other fellow humans – in a lot of distressed states of many kinds – so we go and help them. Animals seem to have no reservations. Humans unfortunately do. If they do, some are classed as a brick-block, others are open to being helped. Openness helps. It makes the task easier. Resistance in hanging on to the disease does not help. Some do not want to get better, even if they say so!

The Fledglings Way to Mediumship

I believe the Healing Ministry is a very important part of the Spiritual Truth. There are mediums, and there are a Healer-Mediums, all doing what they should be doing. It is a calling.

It needs your time, your total dedication and willingness to give, but always remember, after all, you're only a Channel, and a Channel only. You don't heal – those on the other side do, through you. You can only give your time, not your energy, otherwise you would deplete yourself – and one must not do that! A good Medium, a loving, caring one, should be a good Healer too. Not everyone wants to be a Healing channel as well. Free Will operates over all things. You must choose! It takes a very special person to be a Healer, and to see all kinds of sufferings, and go and give their time to alleviate some of it, at least. Mediumship is a gift, so is Healing. One must use all that with great care and understanding. Never ever try to misuse these gifts. Mind you, very few would do that.

Where there is a cause, there is an effect, but to have bad "karma" is not desirable. One must go about in this world with one's head high, to reach for the sky, and also, at the same time, to keep one's two feet on the ground. This is necessary for Mediumship, and also for Healing. After all, you are the go-between in our two Worlds. Be nice to all people who cross your path. They are sent to you for a reason. It is difficult to be very sympathetic towards some people who are not so nice. But if you deliver the right messages to this type of person, in the end they melt like butter, and surprise you with a great many thank-yous. Never judge a book by its cover. You do not know them. We can't afford to judge, because we do not want be judged either. To keep going, study on your feet! That is important – and to help, that is even more important. One must have the right balance.

Sometimes Mediums and Healers burn out quickly. You must

maintain your own health. How can you help others otherwise?

It makes sense to look after your earthly needs. For your health, take some vitamins. I recommend B6 and B12, selenium, silica, zinc, and vitamin C. A good balanced diet is a must. Get fresh vegetables, preferably from the local health shop (or store). Spinach is a healing food, also carrots. It is getting to be common knowledge that certain foods heal, and others will nearly kill you. A vegetarian diet is a very good idea, especially for Mediums and Healers, because we can't eat those who we love – the Animal Kingdom. It is a sacrilege! Well – for some, anyway!

It would also be very unethical, to say the very least. You have plenty of other food to eat. Why do we have to eat each other? Cannibalism should be over by now. But no, there are still meat eaters. When I see them, I know also I can segregate the humble vegetarians from them. They are far less aggressive, and much nicer people to be associated with.

It is very easy to live by the book, because it should be second nature to you. If not, there is a problem! We should try to be better people than our contemporaries. Self-improvement should be No. 1 on our Agenda. Make a list of what is important to you in Priority order. It will help you to reach your goals, and to simplify your life.

You should make plans for yourself, not too far ahead, but to create reachable goals, and achieve them. Nobody wants to live an empty kind of life. There is no point in that. Always fill your days with a thought for others, and your very own kind of prayer, if you're a Medium or a Healer, or just a seeker for truths. You may find some of the answers, but not all of them. You may not be able to make any sense of it at all. Don't give up hope! Hope is a golden rule to live by!

Live for the light – don't falter on your chosen path. You are on the right road wherever your are, and if you understand that, you will really know.

The Prayer

Great Spirit of the Universe, you see my need and I know you can help me to strengthen myself, and give me my health, to achieve my goals in this Life. Thank you. Amen.

Healing Prayer for Others

Great knowing, everlasting, Infinite Spirit I am asking for healing for _____ (name added) or _____ (names) I know you can help me, and give me the strength to help others. Thank-you, and my thanks go to the helpers on my side, because I never Heal alone. I am not the Healer, only the Instrument in the divine Healing order. Amen.

Our Life is an Open Book   But We Write the Pages!

CHAPTER 39

HOW TO SIT WITH A MEDIUM

Come with an open mind, and expect all, and expect nothing. Be friendly, and do not offer any information. The Medium does not need your help. There are helpers from the other side who are bringing your loved ones through. Try not to concentrate on a particular person. May be others are available, and are wanting to have their presence known. Validate their effort. Thank them for coming. Come in a fairly relaxed state of mind. Wait until the grieving process is over, so you will not hinder them.

Let them come, and let the Medium get on with the job in hand. It is help enough to communicate with the very clear 'yes' or 'no', just to give strength to the Communicator, and not the Medium.

It is imperative to be honest and truthful with a Medium. If you do not understand the message, say so! We can ask for more information, not from the sitter, but the loved one who has bothered to come, because they love you, and care for you, even though you have had problems with them while on Earth. That has passed! They have learnt and have progressed on the other side of the Veil. So forget the previous bickerings, or whatever else! They come of their own free will. Be patient! You will get more. Never interrupt the Medium! If you wait you will get more!

Every Medium works in a different style or fashion, and all of us have our very own jargon.

For instance, Anniversaries are Birthdays. Death means birth, also it could mean some Linking with people on this side. The more prepared you are for the session, the better it will be. Your thoughts illustrate your present state of mind, which can affect the sitting, or session. Please do try to be in a fairly good frame of mind, and be polite. Very few people know how to sit properly, and that is so important for the Communication. Do not try to test the Medium. The Medium is just trying to do the job properly, and without the possible interference of your negative thoughts, if any. Do not be critical, it is not the Medium who is giving you the message, but your loved ones. Do not blame the Medium if what you have had was not what you had hoped for, but only some of it, not all. Even so, you may not want to accept the past details of some part of the message. You can check the facts, so you will find out the truth anyway. It is not in the Medium's interest to make up anything that comes from the Spirit World. Most Mediums are very honest people, and have learnt how to channel the information through many years of development in serving the higher life. All that is asked of you – have patience! It always pays dividends. It may be strange the first time when you go and see a Medium, but it will become easier the second time around.

You will know what to expect, and be happy with whoever is able to come to you.

It is not as easy as it seems – a good sitting, a good session, is priceless!

I am sure you will agree with me. Good hunting for the right Medium!

CHAPTER 40

A MEDIUM CANNOT BE EVERYBODY'S MEDIUM

Some Mediums may give you all the names, and another all the Conditions the Person passed through. All Mediums are working on a different Level, and, accordingly, are given different information by the Communicator from the other side. They do reach out – but in your quest you should be sincere. Mediums are always Learning! It does not matter how accomplished they are. Each and every one of us, I believe, still wears a big 'L' plate.

One day you might be able to give absolutely everything, depending on the Communicator, and another time it can be really hard, if they find communication difficult. Some people haven't got much to say, anyway. They are the same over there, as they have not changed. Some were good communicators here, so they can give you all they have got to say – even help in matters bothering you personally. If they see fit they might divulge a bit about something in the Future too – but they do not interfere – it is your life, so it has to be your choice – your "free will" – you are responsible for your Life here and now, and every deed you do here too. It is the price to be paid – not necessarily with money. Your pride, your ego might suffer, but the only way forward in this world is to learn mainly by hardship. Sometimes the lessons are harsh. It is as it should be. We all have our own vocation, and it up to each and every one of us to try to find it. It is easier here; to learn in the physical world. When you get to the other side of the Bridge, things are very different. But the real Learning has to be done here, on this side of Life. Once we all understand that, it will help us to evolve at a bit faster rate.

It is not easy to be in the Physical World. And in the Physical Body, but we are here for a very good reason. We have to try to learn as much as we can in the short space of our lifetime.

You can live to be over a hundred, but have you learnt that important lesson? You only find out when you have crossed over. For a more evolved Soul life is a never-ending search for the good, the God force. You know there is something missing. Even so, you can't really pin-point what that is. We all want happiness and love, wealth and health. The question is do you deserve it? And if not, you will not get it! Natural Law plays it's part.

You cannot have what you have not put in! That's "Karma" again! The good old story of "cause and effect". No one can escape that Law of the Universe. If you don't pay now you will surely pay later! My Personal Philosophy is 'do as you would like to be done by'. Another phrase for it is 'Be good. Be honest and truthful. to your own self '. You can perhaps cheat others, but you cannot lie to yourself! You alone know the real Truth. Try to be kind to yourself and to others.

Our Life is an Open Book   But We Write the Pages!

CHAPTER 41

HOW TO SEE A SPIRITUAL HEALER

What to Expect?

All Healers are not the same. Some are working in full trance, others in a semi-trance, or just in a higher state of consciousness.

One should always meditate before a healing session.

The patient should come in a fairly stable mind, and sit in a comfortable chair. There is no need to remove any items of clothing. Healing penetrates walls, so why not the garment one wears?

Music helps the healing process. I work with music – not all Healers do – it is a personal choice. I found it is good for a nervous patient, or for anyone to unwind and relax. Let the Healer take over!

What should you expect from one session of Healing? Well that depends what is wrong with you. One session helps, but I would say for a cancer growth to shrink, it takes quite a few sessions. With "Aids" it takes time to get the red platelets up again. For a knee pain you might be blessed with only one session. The same applies to a bad back – but not always!

The more you can relax, the easier the healer and the

Healers Guides attend to your special problem, penetrate your health Aura.

I do not believe in touching. Harry Edwards, the very famous Healer, did. But, then again, we all work in our own unique way. Just be part of it – you don't have to believe anything – it still works! You don't even have to be religious. It is not Faith but Spiritual Healing! It comes from the Spirit World, with our Healing Guides doing the actual Healing. I have Dr. Bell who is working with me as one of my Guides. He was an Ear, Nose, and Throat Specialist while on Earth. I had a hard of hearing Lady – she came the first time, and on the second she said to me "Don't shout!" Bingo! One session removed the inner ear canal deafness problem for good! If we find the right Healer for you, you will be laughing, I believe. Many good, if not excellent registered Healers are available from the N.F.S.H., but you can find many others in your local area. It is a question of seeking and finding, really. Also there are colour healing therapists from the Maitreya School of Healing.

Maitreya means World Teacher. As you can see there are many concepts of Healing.

The important part of any healing is to help you for whatever you have chosen, also whoever you have chosen.

Our Life is an Open Book   But We Write the Pages!

CHAPTER 42

PSYCHIC OR TRANCE HEALER

That is different – like Stephen Turoff or Jeff Boltwood in England, who are doing wonderful Spirit Operations, and, of course, the great lady, Irene Sowter. She includes all kinds of animals in her healing activities.

I don't think there are many Trance Healers in the USA, Australia or Canada – at least I have never heard of them. There are many in the Philippines however. Usually a Spirit Surgeon operates through the Healer, even for Instrument surgery they use a knife, or whatever. But most of the time they are working on the Etheric body, not cutting through the physical body. I had a personal experience with the scalpel operation, as Stephen Turoff operated on my back some years ago. I have never had an occurrence since! He works with a Dr. Kahn, an Austrian Neurosurgeon. I have even seen ectoplasm on his hands when he went into a full trance while operating. His wife, Kathy, assists in the operations.

Psychic News, the National British Spiritualist weekly, can help with all enquiries to find the right Healer for you.

In the USA the *National Spiritualist Summit* monthly does the same.

The Americans Spiritualists do weddings in their

churches, and Funeral Services also with their ordained ministers. Most people Mediums in the USA are called Reverends. This is not so in England – they are called a plain Medium. In the USA a Medium is called a Psychic, which is not so in England. A Psychic in England is not a Medium, even so, that person is good in their own field. Anyone who has the ability can develop as a Psychic, but a true Medium is born that way, and not made! Many are called, few are chosen! That is very true.

It is a very hard path to be a Spiritualist Medium, but the rewards are wonderful when we can make people smile – and they can forget a little bit of their own suffering. We open their eyes to other possibilities, and other dimensions, and we can see the immense relief when your wonderful communication wipes away the tears. We see also the tears of joy, and we rejoice with them!

Try to be a happy Medium! We must seek balance at all times, after all we are here in the physical world learning our lessons too, and we should never forget that! Life is very important here and now, and, of course, ever after; but we are here now, and not there yet. So be part of the eternal today, because your tomorrows depend on what you do today. Life is building, life is growing, and learning from everyone we meet, and all we do. When we have learnt all our lessons we get the call that it is time to go home. We make our Spirit return. This is all well planned for every one of us. Trust God, the Universe and yourself in all that and what happens to you here serves the higher good – the Godforce, your Higher Self, your true God-like self.

Life is a short journey, so work on yourself. Give, and don't worry about receiving so much. Accept yourself, and accept people around you, whoever you come in contact with. So there is no man or woman in this world from whom you cannot learn something from. We are each other's teachers. Keep your head high if you're a Medium or Healer, or just the one who is seeking the Truth. Go on doing your daily duties, be happy, and if not, at least try to be content. You can change your life as soon as you can see how you can. There is always a way out of any given situation.

Believe you're here for a reason, and you're a wonderful person, because there is only one of you in God's Earth plane. You were unique, and so am I. All of us are wonderful, because there is only the unique one of us running around in this world.

Try to look for beautiful things, and beautiful people, as it is all in the inside, as you grow in Spirit, you will find like attracts like! So you have nothing to fear, except fear itself. Be brave, take things easy! Work hard, play hard. Life is a controversy, and each and every one of you have to find your own way in it.

Invisible friends are helping you. Your protectors are around you, so you really, in truth, never ever walk alone! I ask the Universe, The Creator of all, to help you in your Progression to find the truth for yourself, and find yourself first of all!

I wish you, dear reader, love and a light, and the wisdom to be able to give, and not so much to receive.

It is all in the giving!

Blessings will follow your sometimes faltering steps.
The knowledge will strengthen you to strengthen others.

To hold in your heart dearly those who are near and dear to you, and those who are far away, but with you in thought and love.

And remember always to give love to all, help of any kind. Be kind to all animals. They are God's favourite creation – and be nice to yourself! Love yourself, and like, even if you cannot love, all. After all you're here in the melting pot. You should always remember you are human; but do not make excuses because you are. We know that. The Higher Power knows it too well – be brave, put on a smile, make others smile on the way, and the Force be with you always, to show you the way.

As I always say – Love and Light in crystal clarity will show you the way, but do not forget to ask – Love and Light.

Our Life is an Open Book   But We Write the Pages!

CHAPTER 43

THE ETHERIC

The Eternal Light shines on you forever. You are God's children, and you will have all Eternity to be with the Shining Ones, when you advance to that stage in the order of things.

The Spirit Side is a well-ordered place; there is no chaos either now or when you graduate to the Higher Order upstairs – the Spirit World, the Kingdom of Heaven, God's paradise in the everlasting life.

Our Life is an Open Book   **But We Write the Pages!**

CHAPTER 44

WHAT IF?

What if the spirit world was not above, but very close to us?

What if our loved ones are so very close most of the time to us? If we would only have that knowledge? What if all of us, not just Mediums, would be able to commune with Spirits most of the time? What if God would walk beside us, and not just our Spirit Guides? If you call for help it can be heard, because they are only a thought away. What if Life would last forever? It does! The shape will change only, not the spirit within. Our Spirit self forever remains the same, and that substance lasts forever.

What if you are indestructible? You are! In the higher planes you go on for sure. Life is a gift, and it is everlasting.

What if all our accumulated knowledge has been compiled elsewhere? It has! You can browse through books that have not yet been written! In the Spirit Side you see through forms which have yet to become a form in the solid earth sense. We exist in a parallel Universe. We live nearly side by side – at circle within a circle level – like step-like, of course in the earthly sense only.

The brilliance of the Spirit outshines anything on earth you care to think about. And if you stretch your arms high enough you can touch the stars!

Our Life is an Open Book   But We Write the Pages!

CHAPTER 45

WHILE ON EARTH

Do meditate. We all need that to participate in the activity we call Life. Do remember to do some good every day. Remember life is temporal, and you are mortal in the sense of the Earth plane. You are here for a short time only. Don't struggle! Be brave! Take life as it comes. Give yourself treats when you deserve them. Aim to learn much. Whatever you plant here the seed or thought will flourish forever in the soul of another. Aim for balance in your life. Aim for Greatness of your Spirit self. Aim for growth for your soul – at your journey's end that is the only thing that will be counted. Always lend a helping hand. Don't wait to be asked for it – in that way you have helped twice! Try to be yourself at all costs, after all you cannot be any one else. Life is an apple, green and needing to be ripened – when the apple has ripened it falls to the ground – the same with humans. Life is a journey – the journey of the apple – the seed comes to bloom, flowers, and then dies! And then you replant the seeds, and the cycle goes on and on.

The cycle ends in the Spirit World – metamorphosis takes place. The caterpillar becomes a beautiful butterfly, and has wing so it can fly. So can you – by thoughts alone. Do you know what real freedom means? If the answer is No – you're wrong. Freedom means you have got wings without having to have them. Freedom means you can travel by thought alone. You can build by thought alone. And the oneness with the God, the creator, and the real you provide a long lasting relationship, a most important partnership, which will last forever! I wish you a pleasant travel in your soul's journey – the best in your life!

Our Life is an Open Book   But We Write the Pages!

CHAPTER 46

THE DIFFERENCE BETWEEN A PSYCHIC AND A MEDIUM

It is quite a big divide between a Psychic and a Medium. In the U.S.A. a Psychic Medium is a Spiritualist Medium. In England a Psychic is somebody who works in the much lower vibration, on a very different level.

A Psychic is someone who can be able to sense things, and is quite intuitive. Don't forget there is only one of everybody, and no two Psychics ever work alike. Everyone develops differently. Some are quite happy to read the tarot cards only, sticking strictly to the meaning of each card. A better quality Psychic only uses it as a jumping board, and takes off from the cards, using them intuitively – hence intuitive card readers. There are no hard and fast rules here. All is open to the individual's own interpretation. I believe this is the best way. The Psychic has learnt to use his/her Higher Self, and is able, and capable to see the past very much in the present, and the future too. Unlike this kind of a Psychic, one can use the object-reading method called Psychometry.

Our Life is an Open Book   But We Write the Pages!

CHAPTER 47

AND NOW WHAT ARE YOU DREAMING ABOUT?

People dream about all kinds of things. I hear the oddest of dreams any one can hear about.

You can watch your dreams. You could try to remember them, and write them down. You might be getting messages in your dream state. We all do. Some people remember them, some don't, but, nevertheless, all people dream. All animals do, too.

Your dreams are a map of your inner feelings, your fears, your worries. But they all come as images, and a bit clouded, sometimes.

You can fly in your dreams. It is usually an out-of-body experience, a concentrated out-of-body experience, or an Astral Projection, but they still belong to the dream. Even so, there is a very different feel about it. Psychics can do it easily. I have mentioned about Remote Viewing in another chapter. Yes, you can form your own mental telescope, and see what is going on in Australia, or go to Las Vegas, and see the Strip. You can be part of it, or wherever else you want to go.

You can visit other people, or friends, any time – it is easier at night. You can pop in, have a look at what they're having for dinner, or whatever else you want to view. The choice is yours – once you have learned the Art of how to do it.

You can't disrupt privacy. That is not allowed by Natural Law! You can't send bad things – they bounce back at you then a thousand-fold! But any fool knows that! If not, don't even try that anyway, you'll only get badly hurt. Don't forget that!

Our Life is an Open Book   But We Write the Pages!

CHAPTER 48

SPIRITUAL MEDIUMSHIP

To serve the highest you have to aim high. You have to be a Spiritual Person. But please don't talk about it – do it!

I have heard many times people proclaiming "I am very Spiritual." Fine! Prove it!

It is easy to live the Right Way. I don't say forget the self – I definitely say, don't forget your Higher Self, Who you really are – a Spirit in essence. That is what you really are, and always will be.

Spiritual Mediums are normal people, with a heightened sense of awareness. Knowledge is either given by our Helpers, Guides, door-keepers, or comes from Spirit Entities, who have learnt and advanced in the Higher Life. We are given Spiritual Philosophy from our Guides, and they do look after us. Spiritualist Mediums are still very Special People; special because they are. We are able to help so many people from all walks of life – giving them something so extra-special – something earthly money cannot buy!

1. Peace of mind.
2. The knowledge there is no death, and we really never die – it is a transition from only one state to the next state.
3. Messages are the most important.

The Way you Work

All Mediums work very differently. It has to be this way, and no other. The more knowledgeable you are, you are allowed Higher Intelligence to commune with you. The more you understand, the easier it is for the Entity to talk to you (and even so, if you do not understand what they are giving out, always say it anyway) and it possibly means a lot to the receiver.

Medium Perfect?

There are no perfect Mediums. No one is infallible. We all do make mistakes sometimes. What do I mean by a mistake? You, the medium, makes it – not the poor Spirit Entity, who tried to get through, so hard, and for so long. You, yes you, the Medium, can misinterpret vital Evidence. My motto is don't make it up – it is not worth doing that, if you are an honest Medium. Just give out everything as it comes. The recipient knows what is meant by the message. So you don't need to ask the question "do you understand?" It is very sad if they don't. And if they don't, don't force things. Mind you, sometimes they have forgotten important dates, but it will come back to them, and they eventually will thank you for it, or not, depending on their human nature, and the particular person in front of you. All people respond differently.

1. You genuinely must like people. Golden rule number 1.
2. You must be a perfected vehicle to commune or communicate, or pass on messages between our two Worlds.
3. Be specific – as much as the Spirit Entity allows you to be.
4. You can't give more than you can get.
5. On the other hand, if you sincerely ask the Spirit for their I.D., they just might be pleased to give it to you!
6. And the most important diamond rather than platinum rule

is do not add the message. Leave it as it is, always!

Be as sincere and honest as you can be. That is the most important thing. Honesty in all things pays dividends also. Please remember that when you serve.

Without you there is no message. That is very true, but you're the vehicle only – I mean only – don't have a halo above your head. Don't think you are brilliant. The Spirit Personality is who is coming through, and not you, the Medium.

Don't have airs and graces about you. You are there to serve – and that is all. Yes, you can be brilliant when you allow the message to flow, and open the door to the Spirit.

Remember to be humble about it all. After all, you are only the Medium, and not the message.

I have to point out that it is your personal responsibility to deliver it well.

It is also your personal responsibility to live life well, and in a spiritual way. In life it is up to you – most things are! Fate plays its part too. Don't let things happen to you, but make them happen for yourself, whatever your craving for. There has to be some kind of an inner hunger for Truth, for the Light, otherwise how can you possibly call yourself a Spiritualist Medium?

Perhaps you should think about that!

A Spiritualist Medium is serving the Higher forces standing for Higher good.

You have to have in you the nucleus to develop that inborn

ability to the highest degree, otherwise do not bother.

Humanity needs good if not brilliant Mediums – the Call is always there. Mind you, many are called and fewer are chosen. I have said that before, but I don't mind repeating it as many times as I have to of the importance of being a good and honest Medium.

We do not aim at Psychisim (only dealing with this Life) – we don't care what you had for last night's dinner. We give Survival Evidence, and do not foretell the Future, except if the Spirit wants to relate a special future event in your life.

Be serious about your chosen path, but not too serious. Don't forget your own sense of humour, and that of the Spirit either. Clarity of speech and a nice kind personality (if you are made of that stuff) will help you.

People have to relate to your Humanity, your human nature, the inevitable ups and downs that all can understand very clearly. Be open and receptive yourself, when the time comes for you to receive information from the Spirit. Don't offer Mediumship to anyone who is not ready for hearing the Truth revealed to them. Leave that to the Spiritualist gathering places that take place in a church, or a temple, or just a hall, no matter.

Cultivate a positive attitude always, and expect to get what you are asking for.

Do meditate before a service. Do not over-eat – you can't work well on a full stomach. Come well-prepared, decently dressed, and always in good time. The Spirits are never in a hurry. So why should you be? Allow enough time to get wherever your are going to.

Always meditate and pray first. Go into the quiet of your soul. Always point out the person in any gathering to be communicated with, and address them properly. Look closely at what the person is wearing, and say "I come to you, who is wearing that yellow jumper, blue shirt, red coat" – call out the colour – and speak directly and loudly enough so all can hear you clearly. If anyone has to strain to hear you, they get bored very soon. Keep everyone interested, even though the message is not for them.

Our Life is an Open Book   But We Write the Pages!

CHAPTER 49

FURTHER TIPS ON COMMUNICATION

Always remember that the message is from a Spirit, and it is uplifting, even though the recipient pulls out a handkerchief. Do remember you are the Messenger, and you represent Spiritualism. Do bring forth Evidential greetings from the Spirit World.

Always remember to be polite, even if others forget names, dates – the human mind is fallible. Do keep your enthusiasm up, and be as positive as you can be – especially with communication from the Higher Spheres. Remember – they are on your side! Always silently thank your Guide Helpers from the other side, and thank them for sharing their knowledge. Close down – that is very important.

Mediums Do's

Come prepared and properly dressed for any service.

Do meditate and prepare yourself prior to serving.

Do indicate the individual you wish to address – by saying "I come to the lady with the yellow blouse", for instance.

Do speak directly and loud enough to be heard in the back rows, especially if it is a Theatrical demonstration.

Do remember that the message is from the Spirit, and it is always uplifting. Do remember that you are the messenger and not the message; and you, as a Medium, are Representing Spiritualism. Do prove the Continuity of Life by bringing evidential greetings from the Spirit World.

Do remember if you are serving in a Spiritualist Church . . . messages are greetings, and not a Reading!

Do be polite to other workers of Spirit.

Be kind to all.

Do be Enthusiastic and Positive, as you are communing with The Higher Spheres.

Do silently thank your Spirit Helpers when you are finished for sharing.

Do watch other Mediums at work, but do not compare any.

What a Medium Should Not Do – I Mean Never – Ever!

Don't think you're the best, and a Godsend to Humanity, because you're a Medium.

Learn, study and remember the laws of decorum first.

Don't ever ask any questions while you are delivering that message. Never ask "do you understand?" Of course they do.

Certain things can be verified at a later date (as I mentioned before).

Don't forget neither you nor your Spirit are infallible. Not everything always go 100% smoothly.

Do remember the Spirit energy has to blend with the sitter's energy. If there are not enough people there, you can feel the energy level dropping. I can really touch it sometimes.

Never ever put down another Medium, just because he/she works differently from you. There is no right way. Only the way to give that evidential message. How you get that is your business and the Spirit's.

Don't get the wrong idea that Spirit teachers do all the work. You have to keep developing yourself. I call it self-improvement. And it never ends!

Be careful the language you use is not obscene, or crude in any way – Spirits do not use that kind of language.

Don't put all the blame on a Spirit Entity for a poorly delivered or Negative message. Watch your own thoughts. Be on your guard all the time!

And don't ever forget you must be Spiritual to attract Spiritual Helpers from the other side. The more Spiritual you are in thought and action, the Higher you attract. "Like attracts like." It is a natural law and no one can change that. Don't say you are a Spiritualist Medium if you only use cards, crystals or tell Future Fortunes. This is as alien to a Medium as chalk is to cheese.

Two other important things to look out for start with a Capital 'C':
    Culture is important.
    Cultivate the right attitude is another.

The Fledglings Way to Mediumship

Read as many books as you can – it is only other people's view of the world or beyond, but you are learning all the time.

Everybody works at their level of development, and in their own very unique way.

I have discussed in previous chapters the different Mediumships.

1. Clairvoyant.
2. Clairaudiant.
3. Clairsentient.
4. Clairgustient.
5. Physical Mediumship.

There are no other ways.

There is "DIRECT VOICE" of course, but there is no Leslie Flint left in England, who was the most brilliant at that very special DIRECT VOICE phenomenon – so, sadly, there are very, very few – if any – nowadays.

No Medium is perfect, but we all have to aim at perfection. Never let your everyday life disturb the communication. Keep an even keel at all times. You can't be angry, and then go and do this type of service. Leave anger behind. Shut that invisible door on it.

Look at Nature – a lot of nature is perfect. Look at the Seas – there is lovely energy there; the ocean, the ebb and flow of the tides. This is your life! In the springtime of youth, you are hopefully learning; in the Summer Time of your Life you live; then comes autumn – the fall. Suddenly you're are not 20 any more. Accept it! Hopefully you will have learnt enough by now to reach Higher, before we go home, and teach others, the young ones who come after us. Winter is the freezing time – stocktaking time.

Look after yourself and do care about others. Be sensitive of the needs of others always. Not just humans, but all Animals. They are God's creatures. I never kill an ant, a wasp, or a fly. I catch them all, and let them out. You did not create any of them, so you have no right to kill them. You are not the creator of any sentient beings. You yourself belong to created ones. Your parents lent you your body. Your Spirit self comes from afar – the place called Higher Life.

You are indestructible. You are beautiful – you are you! And you are meant to be forever! That is a promise!

Look back on your life – was it by design? Was it by destiny?

Have you made the right choices? Or is it bitter and full of regrets? Whatever it may be, you cannot turn the clock back. The Earthly clock ticks away. But like it, your body clock lets you know hunger. "Feed me – feed me!" It lets you know you are tired. You need sleep to feel full of energy all day. You need time to think, time to relax, time to rejuvenate, time for everything. And there is always not enough time to do it all! Time is running out for most of us most of the time.

There are no clocks on the other side, and you are there forever; in that beautiful Summer-land – in the Higher Life – the Spirit World. That is a promise! Kept for all of us that have ever lived over here, and live on over there. The thorns are only here. It is a fairly sad world here, but then again, mankind made it that way. Homo sapiens are not the best examples of Creation.

If people would only use their better nature – but they do not! Greed, hatred, envy are all very negative qualities, which have taken over this side of life. It is very hard to find a few nice souls here who keep the world going, fighting for good. Mind you, Evil is always overcome by Good! You might not find real Justice here, but you surely will later on.

Life begins on the other side, the Higher Life. Life continues – that is a fact! Mediums are standing here to give Survival Evidence between our two Worlds.

I call it "I am a bridge" or the "go between" in our two worlds.

We can't give proof – but we do give survival evidence, just the same, only the words are different.

Our Life is an Open Book   But We Write the Pages!

CHAPTER 50

MEDIUMS AIM HIGHER

We must work on ourselves all the time – no slacking! We all wear an 'L' plate while we are here. But we have to work on our Psyche all the time. Never be too happy about the position you have arrived at on this Earth. In reality we have never 'arrived' here anywhere. You will have to try to link up with our Highest Helper Guides. Don't forget Guides are given to you in accordance with your own knowledge.

When you are ready for it – and you are really Spiritual – in deeds and in thoughts – the best will come to you – you can bet on it!

Our Life is an Open Book   **But We Write the Pages!**

CHAPTER 51

THE WAY OF LIFE

To be a Psychic Medium, but to use the American terminology, is to have a Total Commitment.

Your time is not your own, your life is not yours any more. You serve. It is like entering the priesthood or the clergy, or becoming a nun. You are a Medium – so be it! It is a Way of Life!

Helping others in the best way you know how. You will have done your best!

You lived the life you should have, and at the end of your Earth life you should feel no regret. You should know your Guides are never deserting you, and you never, ever walk alone!

To serve is to give – all the time. If you're prepared to do that, you're a fully-fledged Spiritualist working Medium.

This is your Life!

Your motto should be "I serve, I give, I heal, I mend, I tend – to all who need me. I live in the knowledge that the Spirit gives me, and I pass it on to others."

CHAPTER 52

A MEDIUM'S MOTTO SHOULD BE

I am here to serve. I am a Minister of my Religion. I am a torch-bearer. I am a positive person, and wherever I go I give positive messages – as the Spirit intended. I will not add to or subtract from any message given to me. I pass it on, however I feel, or see, or hear – always!

I am here on God's Earth because I wanted to be here. I am here for a very strong reason. And here I stay, until my time will come to go to the Higher Life – to carry on serving, perhaps as a Guide, for a future Medium here. To take under my wings any new fledgling, and to give it wings to scale the heights, to fly higher than higher. Within my power I will help another to come to bloom, and I will watch over every faltering step of my chosen one here. So let it be!

CHAPTER 53

THE SEVEN LEVELS OF CONSCIOUSNESS ON THE SPIRIT SIDE

The place you call Heaven, or Higher Life, has seven planes of understanding, or consciousness.

When you depart from here you will go to the Lower Astral plane.

The Lower Astral Plane

The lower astral plane is not much better than here. It bears a very strong resemblance to life on Earth. You can still eat, or drink, or smoke if you like – loved ones from the much higher planes will come and visit you, to make you understand where you are, and what you are doing in a place like that.

Slowly the fog will lift, however long it takes. Don't forget you have got all Eternity – not 7 score years and 10. You are OK. You are in the Forever.

The Second Astral Plane

Call it Plane One – one step up – and conditions have improved. The Hall of Learning is there – we learn more to expand our Consciousness Level.

Plane 2 – Level 2

Your consciousness has improved – it is now two steps up from where you have been. The Grail-Light beckons you. The gardens are forever green, and a golden sun shines on you all the time. There is no need for rest periods.

You will feel energised just by inhaling the "Prana", that ozone-rich Spiritual Air. All the lovely animals you have seen on Earth can be seen again on this plane. All the Plant life known to you can be seen there also. Your Loved Ones visit you and urge you now to try to visit them on the higher planes. Once you have gone back to school there, and learnt how to communicate, you will advance at a much faster vibratory rate. All is motion. All is vibration. Aim Higher Still!

Plane Level 3

On this plane you will see all the mineral Kingdom come alive. All stones can talk to you! You will see some dim Auras – around people and things – your eyes and ears will slowly adjust to beauty, and the music around you.

A new guide will be assigned to you, to teach you, and to take you further. The Hall of Knowledge and the Hall of the Great Library will be open to you now.

Plane Level 4

The Light is pure gold now. You see golden lakes and ponds, with swans swimming gracefully on many of them. The trees offer shade – even so, you don't need it. The Auras around plants changed continuously, and you can see at least three or four rainbow colours.

You will see a white bridge. In your mind a question will arise – is that for me to cross? You cross that beautiful white bridge, and on the other side, lo and behold, Level 5 is suddenly there.

Level 5 Plane

I would say Peace begins here from now on, and an even brighter sound shines, but never hurts the eyes. Level 5 is a lovely place, but you will want to go much further than that. You will meet abused Animals who have fully recovered, and also Abused People. Aim for Level 6.

Level 6 Plane

This is quite a high plane, and now you will begin to feel more at ease in your spiritual home. Now you know who you are, and what you are, more than ever before. Now you will begin to understand the God Nature of things. The Highest Good. You will love what you will see – and you will find most of what you seek, or sought after. You will find yourself, your real Spirit-Self – and the wonderful you! Up we go. Next step Level 7.

Level 7 Plane

This is the ideal Spirit World – God's Paradise! The highest Human-Spirit Level – as far as you can go!

You cannot go any further, otherwise you would be dissolved in the presence of the Highest – God's Light – the White Light. You have found yourself – you have attained the highest place in the Spirit realms. You have got everyone with you who you have ever loved and thought lost forever!

You are in your beautiful Spirit Palace now. You will have met your pets (if you have had any) and there is no more separation. This place is perfection itself! Now you understand God's plan for you, and, yes, you are grateful for whatever has been far from perfect in your life on Earth – you now understand what you have been striving for, and have now attained.

You have found Peace and Love, and the harmony of the Spheres – there is music in the air – so bright, so right, so perfect for you!

Your heart is open – your mind is working overtime, it is beginning now – from now on you will create your own reality, your own World – no shadows – only light, so very bright – so light, so very light, and the happiness you have found so profound.

You think it is a dream – where reality starts, or is it a dream still? No it is not a dream. You have arrived at your birth-place – your Spirit home, where you have now originally come back to.

No one will ever wipe away the smile from your face, ever again. You are home now forever! Your loved ones are beside you – you will walk hand in hand.

And if you feel you want to Create, you can paint the most wonderful pictures ever. Spirit teachers show you how to do it – and you'll see the Aura even out-shining from your painting, not to mention from everyone.

The fragrance of scented roses and lilies of the valley are in the air. They smell so sweet, but not overbearing at all. Love will fill the Air.

CHAPTER 54

VISUALISATION

With your eyes open visualise a tree, for instance an oak tree, for inner strength. Visualise the roots going deep down under the tree, branching out everywhere in the depths of the earth supporting that majestic trunk, and that canopy of branches reaching out towards the sky, with the green leaves in full glory.

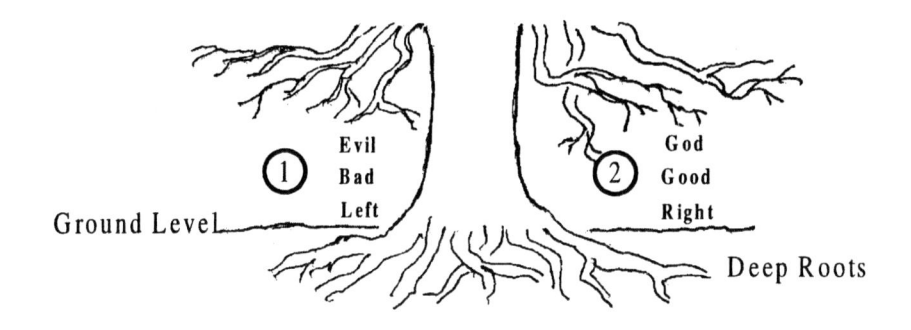

```
                    Evil              God
              ①     Bad         ②     Good
Ground Level        Left               Right
                                              Deep Roots
```

Now separate the tree into two.

One: The tree of God, or good.

Two: the tree of Evil, or bad.

Then close your eyes and try and see what you have just seen with your eyes open, try to start under the ground at the deep root level, then feel that strong trunk – feel the Right side as God – the good side. Try to feel the

Left side as bad – un-Godly – rather Evil; or simply Positive: Right. Negative: Left.

Then go out to try to find a big tree, any kind in the park, and sit under it. Put your back to it, and sense the strength of it. The tree trunk and your back should touch each other. It is Communication with Nature! Visualise yourself growing in strength like that tree, your feet planted strongly on the ground, the Earth you walk on, your head held up, high in the sky. It is the best of both Worlds – it is good for Mediumship, and for your budding Psychic ability. Fledglings grow into birds. You can take flight when you have really learnt the Art of Visualisation, which Leads to Communication with the Highest. Then try more remote Viewing – by Visualisation.

Close your eyes and with a concentrated effort imagine you are going to the Airport to take a flight to any destination you like, even as far as Australia.

Visualise how many feet up the plane travels. Guess the figure. What do you see when you look out from the window? Which countries are you passing? Where do you arrive at? What does the airport look like? What kind of transportation do you take from A to B. And what do you wish to see?

Come and bring back what you want in your mind after carefully gathering the much-needed information. We can view a building, or many – or a missing person – you need only a clear mind link.

Think about it all. Start with Visualisation, but that leads to much more interesting things – there are no limits, and I really mean that! There is no limit for a well attuned and well intentioned mind. No door can stay shut! You can open every door (within limits). The limitations come entirely from you only. You must believe that! All is within you! Nothing is unobtainable, in a Psychic sense. Your Psyche is capable of many miraculous things – well beyond anything you can dream of!

There is a treasure house within oneself. The key is in your mind to open the doors of Knowledge, Consciousness, and Psychic-ability, Spirituality – doors to Heaven, or your own private Hell – you can Astral-Travel, "but that is another story" as Kipling said in the "Jungle Book", one of my favourite all-time classics.

Our Life is an Open Book   But We Write the Pages!

CHAPTER 55

KNOWLEDGE

A little knowledge is a very dangerous thing. How very true that is! You need to learn, you need to grow, you need to know as much as you possibly can. But can anyone do it in one lifetime only? It is not an easy task! If you have not started as a child to read all good classical literature you are already behind – why? Because it is very hard, even with all the time in the world, to catch up at a much later date. Today's youth watch television, and they learn very little from that. You can't really expand your mind that way. You must visualise while you're are reading – imagining things are important to create the character in your own mind. If you have not done that, you must do it later on in your Psychic Path. Visualisation is very important. I don't say you cannot learn that later – you can – but you will find that a hard slog – because your mind cannot see – cannot visualise. When you were a child, I am sure some of you, at least, were able to see things in your head – you have dreamt of fairies, elks, perhaps seen people no longer on the earth plane. Your parents might not have been sympathetic to what you were dreaming about. I was lucky, my mother and grandmother were Psychic Mediums.

We want to learn about how to acquire knowledge. Some knowledge comes from within – other knowledge has to be learnt. We can get that from the Spirit

World if we sincerely ask for it.

We are not talking about Earthly knowledge. It will pass – but the other never passes away. We need the other knowledge more than the learned knowledge.

Spiritual knowledge is the most important thing you can acquire.

Learning is everything – knowing even better!

The knowledge of words is helpful. You can express yourself better and clearer, and clarity is very welcome in Psychic matters.

What you have to say should be clear cut. Never be confusing. People always seem to remember the Negative more than the Positive outcome of anything you have told them.

Travelling helps you to see the world as it is – books to see other people's experiences – but you must have your very own – not second hand knowledge. Then you really are beginning to know. That certain knowing is knowledge, it really is.

Our Life is an Open Book   But We Write the Pages!

CHAPTER 56

ASTRAL TRAVEL

Every night in the dream state you are going out on an astral plane from your body – linked by a silver cord only – and you can fly in your dream state. You can visit places in this world, or visit relatives on the Spirit Side. I have done both, many times.

I have no intention of wasting time by staying put in my bed at night. I find that a huge opportunity to get out – and I do. I have visited the Hall of Learning on the other side – where I have read wonderful books, some not even written yet on this side of life. I have heard music still to be composed later on here.

I meet the Animal Kingdom's lovely creatures, the elephants with their tusks, and those murdered for theirs here – I have help them on the other side – shown them which way to go and reassured them. They are all right now.

These kinds of visits are time-limited. My Guide took me there when I asked for it. You can only ask your Guide to show you the way (if permitted) to see a glimpse of things to come. I have travelled all over on the other side that way, by getting permission to see, hear and to know what is awaiting all of us when we get there.

The Spirit World is a very beautiful place for those who

deserve to get to the Higher Planes, and to the lesser planes for those who did not deserve any better.

You decide, while you are in the Physical body, in the physical plane, with your own mind, what is better for you, according to your own actions, by your own free will – you must believe that! When you Astral Travel, you must remember where you are going, and how to trace your steps back.

The only safe and secure way I know to go about these things is by holding the hand of your Spirit Guide or Helper. The silver cord pulls you back to the physical body, anyway – the only time it is finally severed it is called Physical Death. Then you can really soar skywards. What a journey! What a ball you will have – Freedom at long last! Beyond your wildest imagination!

Our Life is an Open Book   But We Write the Pages!

CHAPTER 57

MUSIC IN THE PSYCHIC SENSE

La fleur que tu m'a - vais je - té - e

Music is good for the soul. It is uplifting – and healing! It is conductive and helpful. It is magical – you can fly on the golden carpet of music. You can really take off! It is important in Meditation. It is good for Readings. It puts you and your client at ease – always! It works its own Spiritual wonders.

Good music calms the soul, is butter to the Spirit – everything flows with rhythm. The music has to be New-Age music, or Chopin, or Mozart. Lizst is good in the background. Never played very loud. It has its own contra-effect. Think of it mainly as low, tuneful, and not making too much noise, but helping you in your concentration, Meditation and focusing. Your mind has to be clear, not clouded with any harsh music or other thoughts. So music is cleansing your mind – the very core of your being.

I used music for Healing, for Meditation, and for Concentration. I can write or paint better with it. Music is colourful. The high C is yellow, brain material, or gold. I was once watching an opera singer, and I saw gold, yellow, silvery blue, pure white expansion in her Aura when she was singing the higher notes. Purple, green, brown with the lower octaves. The Aura always expands with music. Let it in!

It's like standing under a waterfall, and letting the music wash all over you – a shower of music. Yes, I do love music – it is very creative, helpful and wonderful. It is another Spiritual tool – it really is!

What music can do for you, no other things on earth can! That sort of music belongs to the Higher Spheres – I must stress that!

All creativity comes from the Spirit World. All inspiration is linked to the Higher Life! So look no further – look to music for inspiration! The aspiration lies within yourself, but music can be the key to opening it, to tap into your Inner Self. You can laugh, or you can cry, music just touches you very deep down in your Heart Chakra (see Chakras for reference). Music is a swirling energy, like your Chakra. Unlike any other unseen energy, it can be seen by Psychics. It moves, vibrates, and gyrates, and you can move with it.

Dance music makes you want to dance. Energetic music energises you. Soft, low key music can put you to sleep. Melodious music can make you happy (it is just a state of mind – all things are, actually).

All is in the mind! Of course it is – but you must work on it to expand it.

We are all born with some kind of a brain, but the Mind is a Bigger Issue. The larger mind is able to see to the Great Beyond too – not the physical brain. Learning helps to open you up to other possibilities and probabilities.

Not everyone wants to know, but you are reading this book, so you can find your answers here, or hopefully, you can.

Music is untouchable, just like the power of your own Mind – not the Brain. It is capable of many things, depending on the mood of the composition; and of course, on your very own mood at the time of listening, or half listening.

Music is very powerful where a lot of people are gathered together, like in opera houses and concert halls. The very atmosphere of those places can be really Electric. Good music Heals the nerves, building new tissues, making your blood flow better – like a good night's sleep, it is very essential for your well-being. Music is for the body, mind and spirit – all three of them.

You are much, much more than just your body. You have a mind and you are a Spiritual being, here and now, and always will be – within this body you are housed in now – or without it. Your very Essence, the Real you, will never change. I guarantee you that! It is a promise from the Higher Sources. So enjoy the music, expand your level of consciousness, it will take you further in your chosen path – or pathways.

U - na fur-ti - va la - gri-ma   Negl'oc-chi suoi spun - to,

Music is the Essence of your Soul

sotto voce

Va, pen - sie - ro, sull a - li do - ra - te

Our Life is an Open Book   **But We Write the Pages!**

CHAPTER 58

ANGELS, ANGEL CARDS

Angels or Spirit Guides have always been with Humanity since time began.

Everybody has got a Helper in this world, and when you pass from the physical body to the Etheric he/she will probably greet you first, or help you to make the transition as painless as it possibly can be.

Angels, or the hierarchy, contain the four main Angels – Gabriel, Raphael, Michael and Uriel in the traditional or orthodox sense.

Nature spirits (little Angels) are also around us, and because you're unable to see them, it does not mean they do not exist – they do. How many times in your life have you felt an Angelic presence? If the answer is No – you are wrong. The presence who was there where you were born, apart from the one who attended your birth, will come to collect you when your Earth time is ended. Angels, Guardians, Spirits, Helpers, Doorkeepers, Guides – they are all the same – depending on your beliefs, upbringing, country of origin, and what you have experienced in your lifetime. They are shining a Life Force – some of them never having lived an Earth life. Others have, and they have chosen to help you with your daily lives, but not interfering with your "Free Will". They help you in time of severe illness or great danger. They try to give you a warning, but sometimes it falls on deaf ears, but, if you listen, really listen, in the silence of your very soul you will hear them audibly sometimes. At other times, just a thought crosses your mind, or you hear them inwardly.

In Meditation in the Alpha State they do come very near to your "Aura", blending with and reaching out when you reach out in the silence of your Soul.

Quiet is very important. The quiet times in meditation are when you can learn the most. You could try this with cards called Angel cards – just pick one and concentrate on it. What does it say to you? Has it answered your question, or is it something in your subconscious mind, or some word to meditate on?

When I was a student Medium, or, as we call it in Spiritualist jargon, a Fledgling, I remember in Stansted Hall, at the Arthur Findlay College, I had to pick a card, and go up to the platform and speak on it as an inspirational speaker for ten minutes. That ten minutes can be a really long time – but you can get help. Silently send a thought to your Angel or Helper to put the words into your mouth, so when it is opened you speak the truth – spoken from the Light that comes to enlighten our World – to show the way in the darkness. From the Darkness into Light! I have found the hardest card subject is on Synthesis. Why? Will try to speak for ten minutes on that subject without coming up for breath – but the Divine will help you.

Education Card No 1
Write a page, A4 size, on that subject and why it is so important, and how does it help you to help others. Try that.

Release Card No 2
What does it mean to you? All is energy – don't forget that. All is motion, all is vibration, pulsation.

Openness Card No 3
An open mind is open to all. All things are possible. Add in the rest yourself.

Joy Card No 4
The Joy of Living, the Joy of Giving. Very few people comprehend the true meaning of real pure Joy.

A card with no message on it – only an Angel
Meaning? No door will stay shut. Add the rest yourself.

_____
_____
_____
_____

Integrity Card No 5
To work for the Spirit the most important requisite is to be honest. You must be truthful, and able to work with great integrity. Don't bother otherwise.

You will not get rich being a Medium, but you will take your Integrity with you when you live on the Earth plane. You will never have to say "Sorry". Add the rest yourself.

_____
_____
_____
_____

Tenderness Card No 6
Be kind. Be good to all. T.L.C. – Tender Loving Care – is needed especially towards the Animal Kingdom. Add the rest yourself please.

_____

_____

_____

_____

Synthesis Card No 7
To Synthesise – to touch the rainbow in your heart – to be aware of your real integrated self. Add the rest yourself.

_____

_____

_____

_____

Simplicity Card No 8
Don't complicate things, either for yourself – and definitely not for others. Simplify things – Life can be simple, but good. The simple things in life are the most valuable things. The Sunshine, Nature, Animals. And please add the rest yourself.

_____

_____

_____

_____

Beauty Card No 9

Here we are touching on the Inner Beauty, and not the one which fades away so fast after thirty or so years on the Earth plane. So see the Beauty in people, in a wonderful piece of music, in a painting, or wherever else you can find it, in a flower. Add the rest yourself.

Inspiration Card No 10

You really can't live without it! We all need inspiration to live. Looking around it is hard to find it in a City. But you must look harder. Inspiration to write and to compose all comes from the Higher Region I call Spirit World.

Contemplate why you really need that, and add the rest yourself.

Communication Card No 11
This allows you to open up your Heart and Throat and Crown Chakra to communicate with those who reside now in the Spirit World.

Don't forget to communicate with those who are living too. And please add your own comments on a sheet of A4 paper – fill it!

Power Card No 12
The Power of Thought. The power of the written word (not Advertising, even though that definitely works). We are looking in a Spiritual Sense for Power – "the Power within". The Creative Power of thought and action.

Add the rest yourself please.

_____
_____
_____
_____
_____
_____
_____

Flexibility Card No 13
Again, a key to all things. Keep your mind as flexible to all possibilities, at all times.

In whatever you believe in the key word is Flexibility!

Think about that, and write a page on it on A5 paper.

Understanding Card No 14
Begin with yourself. If you have got knowledge about who and what you are, and then you can look at others, and you can understand them better.

Add your own comments on that, and let them be twenty words only.

Strength Card No 15
Sit under a tree with your back to it, and feel the mighty power of Nature. It is well worth a try! Also feel your Inner Strength. Your are always stronger than you think.

God gives you strength when you most need it. Add the rest yourself in 10 lines.

Transformation Card No 16
You *can* transform yourself. For example, when the caterpillar becomes a beautiful butterfly – you can try that! Add whatever other thoughts you have.

Clarity Card No 17
To see clearly for oneself and for others – to have the longer view – Remote Viewing!! What clarity meas to you in 10 lines.

Clarity of mind. Clarity of thought. A clear body and a clear mind.

Add your comments, please, in any way you want.

Abundance Card No 18
When you believe it is your Birthright, it will come to you Abundantly. Abundance in Harvest Time.

Please add the rest in ten words.

Brotherhood Card No 19
One of the Spiritualist principles – "The Brotherhood of Man, the Fatherhood of God and Angels".

Do think on that – contemplate it, and write twenty sentences on it.

Love Card No 20
The power of "Love", the Spiritual Love is to be able to love with "Unconditional Love" – so called – real love is born in the heart, and it never dies.

There are so many different kinds of love.

Add your own thoughts on this.

Compassion Card No 21
To be able to feel real Compassion you become a Healer.

Add your own thoughts on that.

Patience Card No 18
It teaches you to be wise, to slow down, to be able to wait. Especially for Spirit Life.

Willingness Card No 23
To learn from everyone you meet, and every situation you have ever encountered, and are going to encounter.

Add your own thoughts on that in four lines.

1 _____

2 _____

3 _____

4 _____

Enthusiasm Card No 24
It makes a big difference to you, and to others. Add your own comments in two lines.

Faith Card No 25
Real faith is your realisation that you never need to question things, because you know that your own Faith is strong enough to believe it will see you through.

Comments on that in two lines.

Spontaneity Card No 26
Life is Spontaneity. We cannot say 'Stop the World, I want to get off!' You can't. You are here for a ride. Let it be rough or smooth – you are here. (Spontaneous Combustion – when you burst into flames – has nothing to do with this message.)

Your thoughts in ten sentences.

Humour Card No 27
You need that for sure! Without a good sense of humour it is very hard to get through life. Have a laugh!

Your comments on that in five sentences.

Creativity Card No 28
Writing, composing, painting, sculpting – all belong to this activity. Some of us crave that Creative streak. Nobody achieves it easily! Strive!

Add your own comments in any length you like.

Faith Card No 29
Your very own. A good thing to have. If you have real Faith no one can take that away from you.

Your comments on that are important.

Trust Card No 30
First, all Trust God and Trust yourself!

Add your own ideas on that message – a whole page please.

Balance Card No 31
To have real Balance in your Life you need both Spiritual and Material. A combination of the two sees you through.

Your comments on that in twenty words.

Harmony Card No 32
If you have got that, you have got it all.

Your comments in ten words.

Peace Card No 33
Inner Peace. Peace in your Heart, Peace in your Mind, your Life. How can you create more of it?

Add your own comments.

Freedom Card No 34
The Freedom of the Spirit. The Freedom of the Soul. The Holiday feeling! The Freedom of choice – the Free Will.

Add your comments.

Gratitude Card No 35
When all is going well.

Add your own comments in twenty words.

Expectancy Card No 36
In the spiritual sense the less you expect the more you will be getting. Always expect the Best. Positivity!

Add your comments – as much as you like.

Grace Card No 37
"But for the Grace of God go I".

Add your comments.

Adventure Card No 38
Life is an Adventure, and you can even enjoy it!?

Add your short comments.

Courage Card No 39
We all need that for the next step, and the step after that in the Right Direction.

Forgiveness Card No 40
It is really Divine! Always forgive – but do not ever forget. An elephant mind is needed. You learn from that.

Comment in five sentences.

Obedience Card No 41
"Obeyed by Thee".

The Law – the Nature of God.

Your comments – as much as you can.

Honesty Card No 42
As much as you can be. Be careful. Honesty pays dividends most of the time.

Add your honest comments – any length.

Birth Card No 43
Re-Birth. Birth of a New Tomorrow – New Age. Physical and Spiritual Level.

Your own comments in two lines.

1 _____

2 _____

Light Card No 44
The white light. God's Light – Light ahead – God is the Light, and the Light is Linking with the Spirit World.

Your comments on that in two lines.

1 _____

2 _____

Delight Card No 45
To be Delighted, to be Happy, to be Contented.

All your own thoughts on that.

Healing Card No 46
We all need Soul-Spirit Healing. For You, for Others, for Animals. Send healing thoughts towards all – always.

Your special thoughts on healing – any length.

Truth Card No 47
There is only one Truth. You cannot twist Truth. It speaks for itself. What your own truth is may not be another's. We all have our own Truth, or are searching for it

Find your own, and write twenty-five sentences of whatever comes to mind on that.

Efficiency Card No 48
Makes a difference.

Write your thoughts on it at any length.

Purification Card No 49
For your Body, Mind and Spirit.

Write whatever else that means to you in ten words.

Responsibility Card No 50
Life is your own Personal Responsibility. So live up to that.

Add your own comments.

Purpose Card No 51
Of life.
Think about that one! Comments please.

Play Card No 52
Don't forget to take time off for it.

Surrender Card No 53
To your deepest Spiritual Desire. Surrender to your deepest emotions, for good only.

Add your comments at any length.

There are fifty-three Angel Cards in all. Try to speak on them for 10 minutes each.

Our Life is an Open Book **But We Write the Pages!**

CHAPTER 59

LEARN TO BE MORE <u>OUTGOING</u>

You must learn to open yourself up, and to be a much more forward and outgoing person. Everybody likes friendly, welcoming kind of People.

Try to be a Popular kind of Person. It usually comes easily to Air-Signs, and much harder to any others – but you can work on that.

Create the Personality you really want to be. Learn as much as you can from other People, and go out and see places. By sitting at home you will get little pleasure from looking at your four walls, and you won't learn much either. The walls will close in on you, and on your desire to meet the World.

If you are tight-lipped person, learn to loosen up, and say what you mean. Others can't read your thoughts – they are not Psychic. I emphasise that you must be clear-cut in whatever you say and do. After all, you want to be an example to others, don't you? If not, there is a problem there already. Don't be shy – you cannot be if you want to deal with the public.

Learn public speaking and elocution – clear speech, from clear thoughts. Your Physical door should be open to others, as well as your Inner doors.

Awaken your sleeping mind and motions, including all six senses, and emotions. It is important to change yourself and your attitude (if you have one), and all preconceived ideas should go too.

A new dawn beckons, challenge your Soul not to be afraid to meet the World and the people in it — at first at least halfway — and then expand from there further.

If you are a cold person you have got problems. One is born with the inner warmth, or not. Nobody can help you with that except yourself — you can at least give it a try.

There are no exercises for that — just try to reach out towards others.

Be good. Be wise, or at least try to be — go out of your way to meet others halfway.

Do something good for someone. Save some animals. Charities need you. Give money, and, if possible, practical help too. Don't be wrapped up in yourself. Try to change, and it is never too late for that — ever!

You can always turn over a new leaf while you are in this world. This is a Real Test, and a real melting pot for all.

Try to wear a smile (even if it kills you) and be sympathetic to other People and Animals who need you.

You soon pick up the speed you will need for outgoing-ness and friendliness. The world was not built in a day, so give yourself time. You are trying to change, you are trying to be warmer, nicer, more entertaining, more outgoing — good!

The Fledglings Way to Mediumship

You will do well, and soon! I am positive about that.

Why don't you? Come on smile – you are winning for sure!

Outgoing-ness leads to Success ... you are the Master of your own Destiny – always!

Reach out for Greatness...reach out for more richness in your life....and be helpful to others. They will admire you for your interest in them; after all, everyone wants to be appreciated, liked, loved, valued for what they are.

Life is really simple, and it is your choice as to how you make it.

> "You make your own bed
> And you will have to lie on it."
> So make it well. It makes sense.

Our Life is an Open Book   **But We Write the Pages!**

CHAPTER 60

ELECTROMAGNETIC FIELDS

Electromagnetic Fields, you will probably say, have nothing to do with Psychic ability or Mediumship. I beg to differ. It has everything to do with it. Energy fields can affect your well-being, they can upset your sleeping patterns, and make you depressed, or just plain very unhappy. A lot of things can go wrong, very wrong with your life. Your sexual performance will probably suffer. You will have no libido. No energy. No zest for living.

Are you suffering from some of the above, or all of them. In that case we will have to look at how you live.

An electric blanket left plugged in, not even switched on, just plugged in, will affect the energy field. Also timers. Switch them off, or rather, pull them out altogether from their sockets, when they are not in use actively. It is a well-known fact that overhead electric cables can affect you. Yes, that is so! The less electrical appliances plugged-in the better that will be for your well-being. Do watch out for all these excessive and unnecessary fields. Electromagnetic fields can be measured, and you would be very surprised at the extra higher voltages that does exist all around you. The television, when not in use, should be switched off at the socket, or the plug pulled out even.

You can transform your life in a much more positive

way, just by switching your mobile phone, television, or any other unused electrical device off.

Changing the mattress you sleep on it every 10 years, or turning it over every two months will give you a much needed good night's sleep to cope with Life.

Learn to attract Positive Energy. How, you probably ask? Simply by increasing your positive energy.

All is energy, all is atoms and molecules. The table in front of you is not as solid as we see it – nothing is. Before that table was made, it was part of a tree in the forest, a living and breathing thing, a porous living thing, which needed water to survive. Surround yourself with water. It has a cleansing, cleaning effect on your whole being. An indoor water fountain is very helpful in creating the right atmosphere, as is also an aquarium. You would probably need a large one, with eight red fish and one black, for good "Feng Shui", the Chinese Art of space cleaning or cleansing.

You do need natural sunlight also. Learn to switch-off unnecessary lights wherever you can, it firstly it will save money, and, most importantly, you will save your Life. You will live longer and be much happier. The Life Force is Positive, not Negative, remember that!

We all have that magnetic field – AURA or Life Force, call it what you will. Everything is alive – but not always well!

Burn a white candle now and then to counteract the Negative force fields, and, if you have a front garden, plant a couple of fir or Christmas trees. In the back garden have some fruit-bearing trees, a few at the very end of the garden. You need a variety of odours there, and a fish pond with water – if you don't have the fish in it, it is still O.K.

All is energising, and the most important person being you!

Attractive colours attract butterflies to your garden. Your fence should not be more than 5 feet (or 1.5 metres) tall. Otherwise it blocks the energy flow to your home.

All those tips are well worth a thought, aren't they?

So far you have learnt all is Motion as well as all is Energy. Radio waves also affect your mood. Your moods can swing, caused by television waves, which I have mentioned earlier, also from your computer. If we measure the energy, or magnetic field around your PC (computer) it can pass the 60 mark, which is very high. The normal is 5. We don't measure it in decibels, like sound waves. They are electromagnetic fields, and they can hurt your body, mind and spirit, in fact all of you! They are especially active on your brain. You need both sides of your brain, the left for everyday activity, and the right side for Psychic abilities.

Electromagnetic Fields affect both sides of your brain. It can damage your awareness, which is a great pity! If you become aware of this you can do something about it, so your mood can swing to a positive, good one.

Surround yourself with plants, especially in the bedroom. They have a good effect on your sleeping pattern, and on your mood too. Be wise, be vigilant, seek, seek out what is affecting your moods in your life, your decision-making apparatus – your brain!

Be watchful – and, if you feel down within your limitations, and you still feel something is wrong, and it is not the electro-magnetic fields around you, move away!

Any seaside is an ideal place to be OK in this respect. I know we are not living in an ideal world, but do try to change yours, by any means you can!

It is possible! And you're the one who will benefit greatly for from it all. So do it – and do it now!

Why do people feel so good on high mountain-tops? That is easy! There are no overhead power cables of any kind there. So there are no Electromagnetic Fields affecting you there.

I have been to Los Angeles, in the valley part. You feel the pressure there. On the top of the Sierra Nevada mountain range you are able to enjoy its freedom, you can breathe freely and easily, and you feel nearer to God, to your Creator.

Colorado is another power place, especially Colorado Springs, a very spiritual place, without any power lines overhead.

You don't have to look further than the Catskill Mountains, outside of New York State, to feel good. In England, and especially Scotland, in the glens, they are a good place to be. In Austria, all high mountains, especially the Gross Glockner, a brilliant, powerful place, its peak covered with snow, even in high summer!

Salzburg, also in Austria, the "Sound of Music" country, is a brilliant place to be naturally you. Also the Urals in Russia, the Carpathian Mountains in Romania, and the list can go on, and on, but they are all powerful places in their own right.

Peru is also very good too, any part of it. Countries that have a low altitude are not so good. So the higher the better!

Back to Los Angeles, USA, Beverly Hills and Beverly Woods are good, healthy places. Space is important.

Australia is a fine place too, especially Ayres Rock. You should touch that to feel real, positive power. The Aborigines knew that millions of years ago before the white man ever appeared on their soil. It is very sacred to them.

Nearly every country has got some sacred place, ground, hill, mountain-top, to gather strength.

If you can't get to any, just touch a tree, and hopefully, no power lines will upset you. Sit under it, and be at one with Nature, and Truth, and Life. I hope no vortexes, no ley lines or magnetic or electromagnetic fields are near you. Relax!

Our Life is an Open Book   But We Write the Pages!

CHAPTER 61

AWAKENING

What do we call awakening? When your curiosity gets the better of you? When one of Life's tragedies hits you hard, or from just seeing the Light? Some unusual encounters happen, like seeing someone who has just died. You hear your name called loud and clear. Tibetan bells ring. (I have heard them many times.) I have seen someone, as I see anyone normally, except he was standing in the Light, with an out-shining "AURA". In difficult times in your life, the so-called "Awakening" can strike like a golden boomerang.

When you were always looking for something, but you did not know what it was, that very special "Awakening" can give you the answer you were seeking for so long.

Awakening is sometimes very dramatic, like the feeling that goes with the loss of a loved one. It can come out of the blue, or something you always wanted, and always asked for. You have sat in Spiritualist circles and nothing has happened, but all of a sudden, there is a breakthrough – an awakening, and you become aware! You suddenly know what is happening – and you say "Eureka" at long last!

You become aware of yourself. You become aware of others – acutely. It is not always pleasant. Sometimes you feel the crowd......and you want to be alone. You seek peace.....aloneness (not loneliness). It is very necessary to be alone for the awakening of all your senses, beyond the five you already know well. It is the Sixth Sense. It is even beyond the Sixth Sense. It is the all-knowing, without having to search for an answer. It all comes to you......suddenly it all is open, like a book, and you don't have to it to know the Contents.

It is a wonderful, uplifting, elevating feeling; that first encounter; that first knowledge, that suddenly all-knowing feeling. I cannot describe it. Mind you, it is there not to make you happy, that will come later, but to be able to help others.

For God's sake put your aggravation aside. It is not you – but your Helpers who are giving you all that. You are nothing. You're only a small speck in the vastness of the Cosmos. Don't forget that! It is not self-importance which is really important....only what you are able to do with your knowledge. To be aware is to be awakened – but your duty lies to others.

Some want to know more – some nothing at all. Here's a piece of advice for you – do not force anyone to believe in yours. Their time will come, when they want to know, perhaps. It is not your duty to try to convert others to your beliefs. Those who were sceptical, stay so. So why bother? There are others who will want to know. So be it! For the sceptical no proof is enough, for the believer no proof is needed.

The sceptic will remain sceptical, whatever you will try to do – until they will experience something for themselves, and even if it is happening to them, they will still try to deny it. It is their prerogative. They also have "free will". It is their choice alone.

Put it is this way – "Live and Let Live." I am a strong believer of Personal Choice and Liberty – your "Free Will". You choose the path you want to walk on, or not. It is up to you. The Real Opening is not, but give it a try anyway. Homo sapiens is supposed to be an integrated Society of Mankind, and we should be more aware of what is going on around us, but most people are living in a robotic state, and are not able to think for themselves. They are not able to see any kind of Truth. I call these type of people the Sleepers. They are not aware, not awake – there are in a semi-sleep condition. Most people are very Primitive. If you can be moved by Music, Nature, Animals, you are sensitising yourself. It can be a painstaking and painful process. You become hypersensitive, which is necessary for Mediumship development. A Catch-22 situation develops. Now you must learn to be on your guard, and close down when you are not working, otherwise you will, possibly, find life unbearable in your awakened being state.

By now you should know what I meant by self-protection.

It is hard to shut all your senses down completely – all six. Just remember to protect them. Have your own little prayer ready – when outside influences (some negative) are bombarding you.

The majority of people will not understand you – you must make allowances for them. Some you must ignore, to survive all that testing. And the Tests will go on and on. The more successful you get within your own sphere of knowledge, the more bombardment you will get from all sides – that is Life!

Not all is Bliss – but worth Striving For. To be awakened is to be aware of all things, including pain, physical and mental…...not just yours and the world's, but from beyond especially – you feel the way people have past from the physical – if yours is a Clairsentient Mediumship. That is not your choice, but it is in the hands of your Helpers and Guides.

Peace be with you!

Our Life is an Open Book   **But We Write the Pages!**

CHAPTER 62

THE POWER OF THE MIND

The power of the mind is the biggest force which operates over all things.

It is an in-built power, and one that you are born with – all within you.

Nothing outside is as important as your mind – the recesses of your mind (not the physical brain).

You have to listen to the highest within your own self to work for the highest good – the God-force.

Good and Evil have always been at odds with each other since time began, and there always will be a fight between these super-powers, and all within you. You can learn to tap into the good within your Higher Self, and go for it always. It makes sense to do that.

As the saying goes, the Power of the Mind can move mountains. I believe it is true. Yes, you can move all things, and as long as you believe you can, so you shall.

I hope you have learnt how to enhance your mind power.

Don't do anything I wouldn't do. However difficult life can get, stay true to your own Higher Self, always.

I have tried to touch on all the important subjects to

The Fledglings Way to Mediumship

enhance your ability to get the very best out of yourself, and be happy with it. To be responsible in whatever you give out, always speak the Truth. Your Higher Self Higher Mind will never betray you, if you mean to do good!

People will test you, and try you, but, as long as you stick to your own Truth, you will not go very far wrong.

Using your mind correctly and diligently, and wanting to partake in the Bigger Truth, you will be all right. Spirit friends will stay with you, and Guide you on your chosen path.

It can be a lonely path, but really, in all honesty, you will never, ever, walk Alone! God and Guides will be with you always. I am sure they will never ever let you down, the clouds will disperse, and the fog will go – and you will see a new dawn, a new Reality. My blessings will go with you all the way. I Wish You a happy and useful journey. You will need all your great strength all the time – to give – and Rich Rewards will be yours, when you arrive, one day, to the other side of Life.

Be brave. Be good. Try to be tolerant of others, who do not understand you yet, or envy your achievements – you know better.

All Heaven opens up to those who have worked hard on themselves first and foremost, and worked for Humanity to make this world a better place. You will become a torch Carrier – take care how you carry the Spiritual Legacy.

Bon Voyage, and God and Guides be with you always, to show you the way. A speedy Journey, and Love and Light be with you, dear Fledgling.

Our Life is an Open Book   But We Write the Pages!

CHAPTER 63

DEATH

Death is the Gateway to Life; that is our belief. Death is not the final chapter in your life, but a new beginning. A continuation of Life in the Higher, or another dimension.

Yes, it is final, as far as Finality goes, for your earthly vehicle, the Physical body. But not your Spirit Self, which you are. You are a child of the Universe, a child of God – and you remain so.

Death is no final chapter by any means. "Death – where is thy sting?" is a song we sing in Spiritualist temples. Only for a very ignorant mind is death at the end, or for a very materialistic one.

A true fact is that you can't take with you whatever you accumulated here, as earthly possessions.

No – you can't take anything with you. But what did you carry here when you arrived here first? Nothing! So you will go out the same way, carrying nothing, except the good here, if you did any in this Life. You will take with you only your Spiritual deeds, not the material ones. Those are the real things that count over there. All the great philosophers knew that life does not end on this side. We all carry on to Infinity.

Plato had some very good insights into what Life is all

about. So did Homer, Kant, and Nietzsche, whose book "Beyond Good and Evil", can give you a good insight into this subject.

Nietzsche believed in God and good. He wrote about "Free Will". Was he a Spiritualist? Probably.

He had admired Socrates and Descartes. He believed in Life after Death – the Gateway to Life.

He has called us "Eternal Children". I agree with him.

We are all Eternal beings.

We are all born and, yes, we all die one day, just to be reborn to another better life, beyond this one.

Death is definitely not the final chapter!

Visualise a white bridge and you start off at one end and you get to the other side when the time is right for you.

Nothing is so final, so profound as leaving this side, to most people. But you are not most people. You have got a mind and you can think – otherwise you would not be reading this. You want to know more? Good! Keep searching with a torch in one hand, and Fate in the other. Since you want to be a Medium, you will see and hear communications from the other side of Life, so you can live the one here in a more fulfilled way, and in the knowledge there is no Death – only a 'change of the Guard' so to speak!

There will be a change of environment, and a change of scenery, more beautiful than anything you ever experienced in your life here. Peace, Harmony, Love, Creativity, Activity – no one is standing still. There will be no great sleep – you will find a new life, and you live that to the full on the other side.

Death is a myth! Death is a Joke!

Life is a joke, here and now.

You are taking part in a learning process we call Life on Earth.

And, my friend, you are wearing a big 'L' plate.

> "So Death, where is thy sting,
> Where thy Victory?"

> The caterpillar becomes a beautiful butterfly, because God has given you wings.

> Death! Ha Ha!!

Think about that, but how can you possibly understand the Infinite with your limited, finite mind?

CHAPTER 64

THOUGHT-OGRAPHY

Thought-Ography, or Spiritual Photography belongs very much this book.

By thought alone Spirit people can project themselves to 'see' Negative films. Sometimes you can take a photograph of a Christmas tree and you suddenly see your father or perhaps your uncle on the positive, or developed photograph.

I have seen many Spirit photographs. I have got a true story to tell you on this subject, where I saw a dog appearing in one. A lady, who I will call Liz (I have changed her name) had written to me asking me to help her dog, who was a beautiful Alsatian. I undertook a postal reading, as we never met. She sent me a photograph of her dog, Heidi – that was the dog's name. She really needed Healing. I told the lady the dog had been impaled on a spike, after she had jumped and landed very badly. The back right leg was in a really bad state. I sent her healing, holding the photograph, and asked my Healing Guide to attend to Lily. A few months passed. Liz wrote to me, and told me that the dog had now recovered, and any further healing could stop. After two years had gone by the phone rang and Liz told me "you don't remember me, perhaps, but I remember you. You healed my lovely dog. By the way, you told me I would also win on the Lottery, and I have won £9 million. Thank you! Can I come and see you?" I said of course.

She arrived and showed me a picture of an impressive house in Wiltshire, with acres of land, and a bridge across a river running through her up property. But what I saw on that photograph she had sent me originally was, I told her, Lily standing in it. She told me she had bought three horses, having rescued them from near-death. She rode one of them, but the horse always bolted in the same spot, and refused to go any further. That was the exact spot where I saw Lily standing in the photograph. Liz is still heart-broken because Heidi had passed to Spirit at the age of 16, which is a good age for a German shepherd dog. She was a beautiful dog. She still is – and she can be seen on that photo!

Lily needed Healing for some intestinal problems . She is here with me in the picture after healing.. She felt much better, and is now as bright as a button.

The Fledglings Way to Mediumship

Gabriel, "Ollie", the horse, had very bad knee joints, and I sent her distant healing for him to Scotland. He became a racehorse, and is doing well, under a different name in the 1990s!

Another lady showed me a photograph where I saw a head only, a bit of a neck, and a man's face over the fireplace. There is nothing on the wall, except that face made visible by the Spirit Entity. The lady told me that it is her uncle, who, by Thought-Ography (by Mind alone) managed to appear both on the negative and on the developed positive print processed by Boots, the chemist. It had not been tampered with in any way. It was one out of a shot of 36 on the roll – but he managed to be visible only on one of them!

Well, by thought alone, we can move objects – by thought alone, they can appear on photographs! The power of the mind is stronger on the other side than here!

We only use roughly about 10 per cent of our mind here (not to the brain) but we could use much more of our brain power if we could only concentrate more. The concentration span is about 10 minutes for the average person, and then they start fidgeting – some smoke, others shift about, foot or hand tap, nail-bite, or whatever. If they read they must look up, look away, put the book down, pick it up, or whatever.

You must focus totally on what you do – that is so important! The mind has to be Tamed. It is wild, and it can run riot. You are the master of that most important instrument you have got!

Your mind is the Higher you. The brain is your Lower Self. The Higher Self is capable of miraculous things. Your mind is far 'larger' then you are – and in physical death the only thing you really take from here is your mind!

When we look at Spirit photographs we must look very closely, and make sure it is surreal phenomenon we are looking at. Not a double image, or light defect, or chemicals from the Laboratory, when they developed the film. When we exclude all those possible defects, we are looking at a real thing, all right. I have seen wedding photographs, where that uninvited (but much loved) guest appeared. I call it a Spirit extra, sitting in between bride and groom!

When you see that sort of thing there is no mistake about it! You do see the real Person as he or she was, or still is.

I have seen Spirit cats on photographs, and also parrots. It doesn't matter who processes the film, or which camera can capture the images. Even a very cheap throw-away camera can be used. Thought-Ography belongs to the Spiritual and the Spirit Realms, and you will be blessed to be able to see one of these special photographs.

I see many examples, and I consider myself to be lucky to see

The Fledglings Way to Mediumship

them, or to be able to 'see' them – well, after all, I am Clairvoyant! Not every Medium is. Some are just Clairsentient (sensing things) which is just as valid, but they are not able to see Spirit Entities, or animals residing in a Higher Life. I can!

It wouldn't surprise me if that wonderful lady, Elizabeth, the late Queen Mother, would appear in some future photographs of the Royal Family. I am sure she would try to get in touch with Prince Charles, her favourite grandson, especially as he believes very strongly that Life continues on the other side. It does!

When Lord Mountbatten was assassinated, a female Medium colleague, whom I know, was able to give wonderful survival evidence of this much loved relative to the grieving Royal Family. I will not disclose her name, as this comforting information was only for them, and not for anyone else. That's what I call Integrity.

You may possibly ask why Integrity is so important? Without it, no Medium should operate! We are responsible for what we give out, and what we do not. In a large gathering at Spiritualist temple evenings of Clairvoyance, we cannot embarrass the recipient of the message. We could embellish it to some extent, but adding to the original message would distort what it is meant to really be. Never add to the message in any way! Just give it out as it is. The Spirits know what they are doing. My Guides, my Helpers, know what they are doing for sure; as also the Spirit Entities. We ourselves do not always, but we can try at all times to give our very best, and that is not an easy task!

Back to Thought-Ography. Yes, all things are possible! Always look closely when you look at your photographs. Who knows who might appear on them for a special guest appearance. Be prepared for surprises! What exciting and wonderful things appear in Spirit photographs. Even as a small child I saw things others did not. To me, it always has been the most natural thing on Earth. I have written Spirit-inspired poetry at the age of 13, and two books. They have not been published. I never bothered to get them published. I had many other things to do, writing for the children's radio for many years; and for Opera, as an Opera Critic. I went to Drama School, and studied acting and singing. Once Tito Schipa listened to my voice at an audition, and he said " No, you will never be an Opera Singer." That broke my heart, but I accepted his advice. By doing many other things I learnt to channel my thoughts in a different direction where I was more needed.

Thought-Ography is still quite an unusual phenomenon. It occurs not very often, but it does happen occasionally when you least expect it. As I keep saying, always expect the unexpected! All of a sudden a beloved face suddenly appears to you, perhaps behind the curtains, and the fog is lifted, clouds are dispersed and you recognise the face with crystal clarity. Bless you, all the beloved ones from the Higher Side of Life.

Our Life is an Open Book   But We Write the Pages!

CHAPTER 65

EPILOGUE

Thoughts for the Day – By Now You Should Know Why

Today is a new day and I am full of joy.

1. I am turning over a page. So I can begin.
2. Every day is a good day, even the not so good ones. I am learning from them.
3. My motto? I go forward and I do not falter.
4. If I fail in some of the things I do, I will start all over again.
5. I am Powerful. I am Spirit.
6. Life is a merry-go-round, but I want to get off it, sometimes.
7. To aim high is always good – but you might get dizzy in the heights.
8. You can possibly reach the summit, if you wish to do so, but you might not like it there.
9. As long as you know who you are, no one can take it away from you – your own identity!
10. If you take care of today, tomorrow will be taken care of.
11. The greatest values are Spiritual, and you cannot buy them with money.

Little Gems by Agnes

To live without regret.

To find the Pearl within your Soul –

That is to say

I have lived,

And I have learned,

I have succeeded!

And God be with you all!

CHAPTER 66

APPENDIX. FINAL WORDS

You come into this world to learn the Earthly Sojourn – it is about just that. Not to be extremely happy or wealthy – surely you cannot take it with you. Release your Earthly fears. Be nice to all – learn tenderness. Rich rewards come after a well lived Earth Life.

Be open to all – whatever comes your way. Your own flexibility is the key to opening all doors, either sooner or later. Understand yourself, and do try to understand others too.

Expect the best from yourself and from others.

Life is and adventure. You're here for a journey – but, at journey's end, we return Home.

Have the courage to find whatever you need to see you through, and help others to find theirs.

Take time off to play. Life does not have to be such a serious thing. And do have a laugh!

Healing begins with oneself. Heal the pain that others will inflict on you, purposely or otherwise.

Keep your enthusiasm under all conditions. That is most important to remember.

Try to see clearly where you are going – make small plans, and stick to them. Abundance of Spirit is a Spirit-given gift that is more important than money. To have an abundance of Spiritual Values is something well worth remembering.

Have patience! It helps to handle your life correctly. It will give you strength to see you through, and Transformation will take shape – I guarantee that! Be honest with yourself and with others. You can't fool yourself! Try forgiveness as a life Elixir. It prolongs your life. And please cultivate your sense of humour. Spirits have that – so why can't you? Learn to laugh at your own shortcomings and those of others. Strive for more Balance in your life – and do try to give that to others.

The power is within Oneself – learn to tap into that great power. Be compassionate towards all living things. Try to Love from your heart, and feel what true love means – you must try to find out.

The brotherhood of Man means we are all human beings searching for something. Don't waste time. Keep a tidy home and mind, and be efficient in what you do. Search for beauty in this world. Seek joy in simple things – those are the real things. Search for the Truth, and, hopefully, you will find what you're looking for. The Truth is out there. Be delighted with pure things like sunshine – aim for the Light – and God's truly wonderful Light will shine on you – always! Be grateful for what you get, and don't forget to give thanks for it. The Freedom you seek is in the mind, and you can take off, by thought alone, on the Golden Wings of flight of the Knight. I wish you a very happy journey by Astral Projection. Cultivate the willingness to share, to learn to grow – Life is Growth!

What is the purpose of Life? You will not find the answer for that on this side – sorry! Surrender to your Higher Self and be the someone you can be!

Spontaneity makes a difference! Believe all things are possible, always! Be creative, any way you can be, and do not neglect your Responsibilities as to what to do with your Life.

Seek to inspire others, and yourself, and do live and work with the greatest possible Integrity.

You have to aim at peace of mind and harmony.

Simplicity is your key – educate yourself and help others do likewise. It will make a difference. And you will bask in the grace of God.

Death is only rebirth to a new life. So never be afraid to 'die', so called. It is metamorphosis only.

Trust that the Great Spirit takes you where you should be.

Find your inner peace here and now, and find yourself.

Abide by the natural laws that govern the universe. Have faith in your Spirit Guides, Helpers and yourself.

Synthesis leads to better things.

Communication with the Higher Realms is a fact. Try your best to attain it, and you will come through life as if purified by Fire – but the Victory will be yours! All I can add to this now is God be with you, dear reader, and fellow striver – God speed, and victory!

Love, Light and Progress in every way be your Guide and Helper, my friends – and I ask for you to be able to see the Truth for yourself, and to help others with your God-given gift.

Before I finish this book I have to add that people always have been afraid of the unknown, or "occult". And there is nothing occult or hidden in being a Medium or a Psychic. When you are ready to practice doors are opened, and not before. It is all in Spirit time, not yours. You might possibly feel ready for the task ahead, but if the Higher Power think you're not, then you must wait patiently to become an excellent Medium, and it is really hard work! Your attainment, your Vibration, is the most important key to open the Highest door – your Crown Chakra. Learn as much as you can – ignorance is no Bliss if you want to serve the Highest I call God, and his Spirit World. All you can do is meditate, contemplate, be nice to all you meet, be helpful to all who ask you for your specific help. You will then be the right Medium for them.

There will be no shadow of doubt in your mind as you will know that Spirit Helpers are with you all the way, and will never abandon you, ever. God is Great, and you are Great, because you are a Helper for the Spirit. You are unique. You don't work alone, but, without Spirit presence, you can't even open your mouth!

Trust the Spirit. Trust your own abilities. But above all, trust God, who you work through, and is your very being.

Your heart must be in whatever you do. Your mind does not come into it, and should not. In pure Spirit Communication all, I emphasise all, knowledge comes only from the departed Entity. I mean that! Your mind should be free, or pure; putting aside personal problems. By putting away yourself, only then can real communication take place, in the purest form. It is very necessary to devote years of study sitting in a circle environment, and patience is also really needed.

The Fledglings Way to Mediumship

Sitters, like Mediums, will come in many shapes and sizes. Some will be very impatient, some will be less so. Others will want to hear only what they want to hear – not what you say! Some will listen, others will not. Preparation is needed before you embark on that journey to serve, believe me. I have had many years of experience behind me, over 30.

You have to be very polite to all, even so, some sitters will demand what they want, unfortunately you can't give it, or not at that point in time. I have to explain "Please wait. Give me a minute." See if someone will bring that person through. Never be afraid to be totally honest. People will respect you for it, and hopefully, understand what you mean. You must make yourself very clear at all times – there is no room for so-called hit and miss from the other side. If it is not clear to the recipient of the message, ask for more. The Spirit is usually willing to make it crystal clear what they want to convey – if they want to.

Nothing is hidden to those who are willing to learn, listen, and leave an open door – open always. All is open, if your mind is left open.

The same applies to Mediums and the sitters.

Do not start working before you are ready for it. Only work in a receptive state of mind. If you're not well, cancel an appointment. It can make you more ill trying too hard in that state.

The sitter should learn to sit properly. Do not expect too much, but expect everything to be open and calm. Don't speak – a simple yes or no is sometimes helpful. Don't give away anything. A Medium does not need your help, ever! You are the one who is there to be helped. The Medium's own Helpers are present anyway.

If you are very recently bereaved, please wait a few months, as too much emotion holds some Spirits back. Also do not sit with your arms or legs crossed, please. Sit in a comfortable position, and just listen. As soon as Survival evidence comes through, just please acknowledge with a yes or no. Your voice vibration is an important answer to the Medium.

It is so very important to be a good sitter! A good sitter is a premium.

It is also very important to be an excellent Medium!

All can try, and give their very best, and don't forget, all is open to an open mind.

God be with you all! And the Great White Spirit be your Guide!

Agnes Freeman

Our Life is an Open Book   **But We Write the Pages!**

CHARLIE.
AGNES FREEMAN.

A Spiritual Story.

CHARLIE
A STORY OF A SPIRITUAL LIFE

by

AGNES FREEMAN

© Agnes Freeman, 2003

FOREWORD

This is a factual story where all the names have been changed. I thought it was necessary to do so. Let God and Spirit guide your steps, dear reader, and the Eternal Light should shine on you always.

Without hope and love in your heart you cannot go forward. Live your life the best way you can, not forgetting others, and especially as we are all brothers and sisters under the great canopy we call Life. Nor do we forget our younger brethren – the Animal Kingdom – all creatures great or small need love.

The Universe is built on this love, and humans must help not to destroy it by right action and right living – by giving Love, which is forever – eternal and mighty.

Charlie was born in 1900, on the 3rd of June to be precise, in the very dreary East End's Mansel Street, near Farringdon Station, London. There was a lovely old pub in the corner, "The Fox and Parrott", along with the corner shop. Always the corner shop where the credit had run out a long time ago.

Charlie's father was a working man. He delivered beer barrels around the East End of old London town. He loved his shire horses. They always made a lot of noise clopping and clapping on the cobbled streets, especially late at night, when the noise was louder because of the stillness of the streets. The street lights were lit by candlelight, and Charlie loved to watch the dancing lights. When he was lying down looking up to the ceiling he was able to see beyond the walls and to the stars, and beyond Aldgate, a landmark. The old train was going noisily about its business above the ground, shaking the whole collection of red brick houses where they lived.

Charlie played with his marbles. Oh, they where lovely coloured balls, and each had a name. Charlie was a very imaginative child. The old man, his father, George Michael Charles, had no idea where the boy got it from, nor did his mother; the frail Mary Ann. Mary Ann's mother, Charlotte, lived with them, and she was a very wise old lady. Despite her tiredness for life she was a wonderful cook, and prepared all kinds of meals on a shoestring. On special occasions they had spotted dick!! Generally their diet consisted of mainly peas and mash potatoes. They always had a bit of Gin for the old lady, who believed a bit of Gin did her the world of good, and it usually did.

Poverty was everywhere, along with the musty smell of damp walls, which did little to lift the spirits. They had no carpet, only the rotten wooden floor, which creaked under their foot steps, but they got used to it long ago. The whole place smelt of ale and must. In the corner they had a very old stove, which smelt something awful when they lit any fire, and the smoke got into their eyes. There was a very creaky old bed with an ancient mattress on it – was it made of straw? They had inherited it so long ago that not even Charlotte remembered who had given it to her as a wedding present. Her dear old George had gone long ago. He was her beloved husband and friend. She was good at mending things, so good they lasted and lasted forever! It had to last as they had no money to buy new things. Charlie was blissfully unaware of the great poverty, except when his feet became too big for his shoes, and his feet became very painful. Grandma Charlotte cut the front off his shoes so his toes could peep out and see the world.

Charlie woke up rubbing his eyes and there standing in front of him waving was George, his grandfather. Charlie was born after his grandad had gone to the Spirit side. He had suffered with pneumonia, and in the end it was a fairly quick passing.

'Hello Grandad, are you real?'

'What do you think, my little urchin?'

'Yes you must be. Can I tell Grandmother?'

'No I don't think so – she'd think your fanciful imagination had put me here. Do you understand Charlie?'

'Yes I do, Grandad.'

'O.K. my boy let it stay just between you and me.'

'It will. I love you Grandad!'

'I missed you until now – I promise I'll come and see you often. Do you believe me?'

'Yes I do, Grandad.'

'I will watch your steps my boy, always.'

Charlie had a very grown-up expression on his face when he looked into his grandad's face, and said it would be a secret, their secret, and it will stay that way.

'Oh my child, my little grandson, how much I love you, how much I care about you – you have no idea, and let me kiss your head. I will come again soon. I will teach you things. Goodnight, boy.'

Charlie looked so apathetic, so thin, so small and insignificant in his bed, covered with a very tatty goose duvet.

Morning came, and he got up to wash his face and hands in the small washbasin, and that jug of water felt so very cold on his skin. The room was icy cold, and he ran to the pantry, after pulling up his pants, and that over-washed shirt.

'Granny, are there angels?'

'But of course, my little one.'

'Is it possible that the dead can come back?'

'Yes it is. You've had a dream, haven't you?'

'I think I did, replied Charlie.'

'Eat your bread and drink your milk lovey, and go to school now.'

'I am going. I am ready now.'

'Bye bye my boy and be back soon, don't stay way after school.'

'I promise I won't.'

Charlotte shut the door, and sat down in a low chair, and murmured to herself that maybe Charlie didn't make that story up, maybe all things are possible. Maybe, just maybe, it wasn't just a dream, but real. As real as I am. I am a God-fearing woman – why do I think of that? But if Jesus has risen from the dead, why not all? Life continues somewhere doesn't it? Well, she pondered, what if she went along to that spiritualist church? There was one in Ilford, and the other was nearer, just off Old Street. She reached for her old shawl, and got up from the wooden seat – her knees weren't what they used to be, but she decided she'd make the effort to go anyway. As she set off fine rain began to fall, and the wind had picked up. Her hair tossed in the wind – never mind, she thought, and hastened her steps.

She reached her destination, and on the door it said "Spiritualist Temple". That's it, she thought, and with that, she opened the big brown heavy door, and stepped inside. The room was filled with the sounds of a lovely tune being played on the organ. The congregation that had gathered were all scrubbed clean, but this did not hide that fact that their clothes were second hand, or had been patched many times.

The atmosphere was electric, and there was great expectation in the air. The music stopped, and everyone fell silent. The rostrum was filled with flowers, and just a few pictures on the walls – not familiar to her. An old lady climbed up to the rostrum, followed by another, and they sat down. There were three comfortable easy chairs. The last one to come up to the rostrum was a very distinguished gentleman about 70 years of age.

The first lady stood up smiling and said 'Everyone is welcome tonight my friends, and now Lady Lillian will address you.'

Lady Lillian turned out to be the second lady who had gone up to the rostrum. She was dressed in a plain black dress, with pearls around her neck, like a choker, and a much longer one, coming down about 22 inches. She began her address by saying 'Welcome to our church, all of you who have been here before, and especially all of you who are new to it. My Guide Bearer will address you all.'

He liked to be called Bearer, or Bruce if you like. He was a Red Indian Guide, but he liked simplicity.

'Welcome to tonight's service, dear friends. Everyone here has somebody above, and they attend to greet you, my Spirit Guide Bearer greets you, and brings Love, Light, and greetings to you all. His warm wishes embrace you, and is sending healing rays to you, all from the Great Spirit of all.'

'I come to lighten your life, and to embrace you all, to give you Divine Truth and Light, to bring real happiness into your lives. Today, tomorrow, and every day…..Spirit friends are with you, and staying with you always, and now the long awaited address given to you by Mrs Evelyn Price, our Medium for tonight. Please answer with a simple yes or no when the Medium comes to you with greetings from your loved ones.

'I come to you, my dear lady, in black, with the blue shawl on

your shoulders, pointing with bony slim fingers at our Charlotte.
'Yes' she replied.
'A gentleman here, he says his name is George, and he was a blacksmith'.
'Oh yes he was. He is my dear husband' replied Charlotte.
'He is taking me back in time, and bringing Timothy with him' said the Medium.
'Yes, yes, he is my grandfather'.
The medium went on to say 'He says you have a bad chest, and to watch your lungs, love'.
'Yes, thank you. Bless you!'
'A lady is coming, and her name is given as Morag.'
'Oh yes, she is my mother.'
'She says she was born in Wales.'
'Yes, she was indeed.'
'She says she comes from a family of five.'
'Yes, she did.'
'Aunt Helena and Bella and James, Jonathan and Sedgwick are coming with her. She is giving anniversaries on May 5th and April 22nd.'
'Yes she was born in May and she died in April.'
'Who is Robert or Bob this side?'
'Oh, my brother.'
'She says that he is suffering with the old leg.'
'Yes, he does.'
'An old injury playing up.'
'Yes, it does.'
'The energy is withdrawn now. God Bless you!'
'Thank you!'
'Sorry love, I have to come back to you. George is back, and he says your grandson has seen him. He is very psychic now, and he is growing stronger every day in the sense of sensing, and seeing spirit. He will be an instrument for spirit one day, and a very good one, too. He sends his love to Charlie. Let him know

he is around both of you many times.'

Charlotte started talking to another elderly lady after the service, and she said to Charlotte 'I know too that your lovely grandson will be an instrument for spirit one day. He needs to be instructed in how to do it properly. You see, my dear, I am also a Medium. My name is Marianna. Call on me if you need me. I don't live too far away.'

'I will', Charlotte said and added 'I am worried about Charlie. He is such a sensitive child.'

'He will be taken care of, don't worry' said Marianna 'When he gets a little older he can sit in a development circle.'

'Is there such a thing?' asked Charlotte.

'Oh yes, you shall see him growing up to be a wonderful helper of humanity.'

Vincent walked through the door. He was an ex-army officer, and a real gentleman.

'Take a seat, old chap' said Charlotte 'Would you care for some tea?'

'Yes, please, I could do with that' replied Vincent.

Charlie bounced through the door doing his hoch-schopping. His friend Ted ran in after him.

'Charlie, Charlie stop! I want to talk to you.'

'What for?' asked Charlie.

'Come on, Charlie, sit down.'

'O.K.' Charlie finally agreed. 'Let's go to the pantry.'

'Charlie, do you see angels?' asked Ted.

'Not exactly angels. I do see people who are not really here anymore' said Charlie.

'What do you mean not here anymore?'

'Well dead', said Charlie.

'Dead?'

'Yes, but I do see them very clearly, and they talk to me.'

'They talk to you!'

'Yes they do indeed.'

'O.K., prove it to me.'
'I will, but it is a secret. Cross your heart, and swear to die!'
'I will.'
'You have to be very quiet', said Charlie, 'and we will draw the curtain.'
'What for?' asked Ted.
'For their sake' said Charlie.
'Why do we need the dark?'
'We don't' said Charlie patiently, 'They do.'
'Why?'
'Don't ask so many questions.'
'Why not?'
'Because!'

They sat down by a large brown table. It was rough and unpolished, so it seemed that the table had definitely seen better days. They had bought it in Petticoat Lane long ago. It smelled of fish and pickle, and pickled fish and mussels….all kinds of cockles, and God only knows what other smelly fish! The brown, round, chairs around the table were just the same – old and semi-broken. The polish was worn away, and bits of flaking old polish showed. They had been repainted, but as time had passed, the paint was now coming off in blisters. 'Sick' chairs and a 'sick' table. The yellow wallpaper flakin…the petrol lamp smelling something awful – kerosine– turned down low to save a bit for even harder days. If that was humanely possible – who knows?

Moses stuck out his head around the door, asking 'What are you doing, children?'
'Oh nothing!' answered Charlie.

Moses' father came to England as a slave, and Moses became a free man after slavery ended, and he was just happy to stay in the neighbourhood, and work behind the scenes at the pub. He did the washing up, and cleaned the place so it was spotless – well, take or leave a bit, here and there. The old inn, where he worked, was haunted by disturbed spirits. The old Coach Inn was just around the corner from Ludgate Circus. He had seen folks come and go. It was a busy place where people came to spend a night or two, or just an hour or two. It was open to all possibilities. Some street girls made their living here, and they were happy to hop into bed for a few shillings. Some were murdered there, and their spirits had not moved on. Nancy and Joelle were two girls who earned their living in this way, and poor old Mary too.

'I see you are busy' said Moses 'I will come back later'.

'All right' said Charlie 'We are busy, but have some bread'.

'No, thank you, I must be going', said Moses.

'God speed', said Charlie.

'Yes, good night', added Ted.

'We need some paper and a pen', said Charlie.

'Why?' Ted asked.

'Wait and see', said Charlie.

Charlie put his elbows on the table, and, holding the pen ever so lightly on the paper, and not really concentrating on it, started to write….

> My name is Patrick. I was in a battle in Verdun. A bayonet went through my chest. First World War. Terrible! All died beside me in the trenches, and I was the last to die. It is nice on the other side. My angel, my wife, collected me. You should know we all live, and life continues. I have done my job. Wally is sending love to your grandad. He will understand the name, dear Charlie. Iris is sending love to your mother, and Ellena….

Charlie wrote it all down, and the session ended somewhat prematurely. It was abrupt. Charlie looked at the small window. It was getting darker, and horrible black clouds were gathering in the sky. It will be stormy, and it will pour down, Charlie thought. It did a second later.

The years had gone by very quickly, and the Marylebone

Spiritualist Association formed, and moved to 33 Belgrave Square. It is now the S.A.G.B. of Belgrave Square.

Charlie was grown up now, and past his 16th birthday. It was 1916. Oh, the happier days of gramophone music, and the talking movies. Great, thought Charlie, but he was under no illusions. Half the world was still starving, while the other half lived it up.

He yearned for a dog, but all he had was an old black cat, who followed him everywhere, and he resigned himself to thinking that it was better than nothing. A cat is a cat, and a cat is not a dog, but he will do. Bruno the cat always kept close to Charlie, and slept with him. First thing in the morning… 'Well who is licking my face now?' Charlie would ask and it would be Bruno again. At last, Charlie thought, he's behaving like a dog, so there will be no need to get a dog after all.

'You will have one'.

'Who said that?' asked Charlie, rubbing his eyes only to see the old man who was standing there with a headband. An old Red Indian gentleman, who was wearing three feathers in his headband.

'I am Hawk Three Feathers. I am your guide, my son'.

'What do you mean my guide?' asked Charlie.

'Your helper son, your helper in this life. I saw you when you were born, and I will see you die. When you will be crossing over to the great beyond, I will be the one who will be taking you there. In the meantime, take care of your life here and now. You will do well. You will work in high places, in the King's household.'

'I want to be in the regiment' said Charlie.

'So you shall be, my son.'

The morning was nice and sunny. Charlie walked out of Mansel Street, and onto Commercial Road, to the market. What a lovely market, full of colours and smells. The smell of pickled herrings filled the air, along with the smell of freshly baked bread. If only I had the money to buy it, he thought. The saliva in his mouth touched his teeth, and he swallowed hard. Well that's that for today. He saw people gathering, God alone knows what for. It turned out to be a long queue forming, with people waiting to see if they could get any work that day. He joined the queue, and after a very long time, he came to the end, and it was his turn. The work available was delivering coal. Charlie thought he'd go for it …..better than having to suffer an empty stomach.

He carried the first sack-full of coal to the cart. His shoulders started to ache after only one load. He went back for the next, and the next, until the cart was really full. The man started to pull away the old cart, like a donkey. He walked by it, accompanying the cart, pulling it to its destination. He had to go to the City, and it was a long walk, but he was young and strong, and he did not think he'd have any problems. The next destination was Chancery Lane, and then The Strand, and back to Covent Garden. The old Opera House stood proud, and under the arches and pillars were the flower market and the vegetable market. He picked up a few cabbages for two pence, not bad, he thought, then a few potatoes for a farthing….we can have dinner tonight, he thought. He walked back home, hastening his steps, happy with the cabbages and potatoes.

That very evening, after a full stomach of food, he definitely felt better, and when he fell down onto the bed, and very tired, he had the most wonderful dream or vision. He was taken to a sunny place full of light, and the beams felt good on his skin and face. He saw his great grandmother, Katherina, walking towards him, and Edward, his great grandfather, and the mynah bird appeared, talking, too.

'Hello, Charlie' said the bird.

Hello, to you, too' said Charlie.

All around him were wonderful spring flowers, the bees buzzing around him, the cornfields and the beautiful cornflowers. There were sunflowers, Lilies of the Valley and poppies in the fields. Irises, gladiolas, and sweet smelling yellow and pink roses.

'I would love to stay here with you' said Charlie.

'No, dear boy, not yet' said Edward, his great grandfather.

'No, go home, go back, you have plenty of work to do in your life' Katherina said, with a warm smile.

The vision came to an abrupt halt, and Charlie opened his eyes, and it was already morning. The thought just came to his head that he must see Percy. His shoes needed repairing. He quickly washed himself, and got dressed. All he had for breakfast was a cup of water, and quickly left.

Percy greeted him with a smile. 'How are you today, Charlie?'

'Not bad, but I'm hungry'.

'Take your shoes off, Charlie' Percy said, and began to stitch them up. 'I don't know how long they will last' he said. Charlie made a face. 'I've got some bread for you. Here'.

Charlie grabbed the slice, which was covered with lard, it was very good. 'I need a job' Charlie said.

'You can deliver papers' Percy said.

'Papers?' asked Charlie.

'Yes, go to Fleet Street. They're looking for someone just like you'.

He followed Percy's advice and headed for Fleet Street. He arrived at the Daily News, and went in.

'I hear you're looking for someone like me to deliver papers' said Charlie.

'I don't know, boy' replied a man wearing glasses, and from his wrists to his elbows Charlie could see he was wearing black cotton covers, 'I'll ask Mr Michaels', and off he went. He quickly came back, and told Charlie that they were indeed looking for him, and that he'd been given a job.

'Thank you' said Charlie.

'Don't thank me, go and see the boss, Mr Michaels'.

Mr Michaels was a tall dreary man, with blue, thin watery eyes and slim glasses. He peered down his nose, and said 'So you are the boy called Charlie'.

'Yes, sir'.

'All right, and from now on you are working for me'.

'Thank you, sir'.

'All right, Charlie, you can start as from today'.

'Thank you, sir'.

'Think nothing of it. I need a strong lad like you to carry the papers. Now wages, let's see, 3 shillings'.

'Thank you, sir'.

Or shall we say 3 guineas? You see, if you do well, you can go places here, it's up to you'.

Charlie walked out with a bundle strapped together, and he carried it by the handle. He walked from place to place with it, dropping by businesses that were on his list of places to deliver. Later on he ended up in Trafalgar Square, filled with pigeons, and looked up at Nelson's Column, and saluted him. What a good spot, he thought to himself, and sat down at the bottom of Nelson's Column, undid the papers, and holding one up in his right hand, shouted 'Paper, daily paper, buy now for a penny'. He was there until about 6pm, and it was getting dark. He only had two papers left – he had had a good day, and bought a pint of bitter in a nearby pub called the Red Lion. Once he'd finished, he started walking home at last.

He went to his room, which he shared with Symon, his brother. Symon, who helped out in a bakery, was not at home, as he worked long hours, sometimes all night, preparing fresh bread and bread rolls, ready for the morning. So Charlie had the luxury to be alone in bed, and not have to share it with his brother. He fixed his eyes on the water basin, which stood at the far end of the room, with the washing water and a pitcher of water. He listened, and in the semi-darkness he saw the water pitcher move. He wanted to pinch himself. I am seeing things, thought Charlie; it is not really happening, or is it?

'Who's moving the water?' Charlie called out. There was no reply. A little later he fell fast asleep. He woke up to the sound of water. Someone was holding the water pitcher over the old basin and pouring the water out. Well, that's great, he thought. 'If anyone's there, will you talk to me?' He then saw a young girl standing there.

'My name is Stella'.

'Nice name' said Charlie 'Why are you here?'

'To help you, because you and I can be friends'.

Another friend, not from here, thought Charlie.

The girl heard his thoughts 'Not from here, no, but I have lived here before you did, and I died of T.B. My lungs were very bad. You know it has always been damp here, and this did not help me'.

'I'm sorry' said Charlie.

'Don't be, Charlie, I am fine now. I am living in a very sunny place, and I am very happy. I just came to see you. I like you. My sister is with me too. Raina is her name, and my father and mother, and my grandparents too. I have a dog there, and he is called Dave the Brave. He saved my life once. I nearly drowned, and he nearly drowned saving me. He got old then he died. Then, I suppose, I have died as well – some blood poisoning. The doctor said nobody could help me. They couldn't, but Alicia, my lovely helper, picked me up from here, when I became very ill and died. She brought a red ball with her, and she said to me that she will always be my best friend, just to follow her, and so I did.

'Did you grow up in the Spirit World?' asked Charlie.

'Yes I did' she answered 'I would love to marry you, Charlie, even though I know it is not possible. I will wait for you in the other side. You are my spiritual soul mate, but not for life, for above. Do you understand me, Charlie?'

'I think I do, but I'm not sure. You sound so grown up, and you know so very much, and I do not.'

'You will learn Charlie' she said.

'I will? Good, but what?'

'I don't know, but listen to your guide. Have you met him yet?'

'Yes indeed. I have got a Red Indian Guide. I like him a lot'.

'Well that is good. Helpers will come and go as you grow spiritually'.

'Really?!' exclaimed Charlie. 'Is that good or bad?'

'Neither' she said 'It is just the way things are here. I know that much, but not all of it. Go and learn Charlie, and you will be working'.

Great, thought Charlie, not wanting to voice this, because to Charlie, work meant food to eat.

She left, and never came back ever again. Charlie wondered why, but he was getting used to it. People came when they could, and not when he wanted them to come. Charlie was growing up. He was eighteen now, and he wondered what next? Where to now? What has life and living in store for him, he wondered.

One day he walked to a bus stop, and waited for an old red drafty London bus, which took all the time in the world to arrive, but, never mind, they all got there somehow. He stood there a long time, and then, all of a sudden, a lovely old lady joined the queue. She was wearing a straw-brimmed hat and glasses. She was roughly 5'. 4" tall, but compared to Charlie's 5'. 9" she was relatively small.

She turned and said to Charlie 'Can I ask you something?'

'Yes' replied Charlie.

'I am a Medium, dear. Do you know what I mean by that? I see things, and I know you do, too.'

'Do I?' Charlie asked back 'Yes, I suppose I do.'

'I know, and you will be a great Medium one day, much better than I am.'

'Well, how do you know that?' asked Charlie.

'You see, my dear, they are telling me.'

'Who is telling you?'

My Guide, of course, but you can do that, as you have seen

your Guide. What is your name?'

'Charlie.'

'A nice name, and you will be very well known one day.'

'I don't know. I'm not sure what to make of it' replied Charlie, the reluctant would-be Medium.

'You must go to the Spiritualist Church, to a development circle, and do not waste a talent like yours. You must not fall by the wayside. Do you understand me?'

'I think I do' answered Charlie, 'but do you know where do I go?'

Yes, my name is Mary Osbourne'.

'Mrs. Osbourne, will you come with me, if you can spare the time?'

'I'll take you there, if I have to drag you there by the scruff of your neck!'

'I am coming Mrs Osbourne. I am very interested indeed', said Charlie.

Mrs. Osbourne said 'Hey, the bus is coming.'

So they climbed up to the top deck, and even though it was very drafty, their little chat kept them warm.

'We are getting off now, follow me', said Mrs. Osbourne.

They got off at Hyde Park Corner, and walked through a few narrow streets until they reached 33 Belgrave Square. On the door there was a lovely brass plate, and engraved on the plate were the words Marylebone Spiritualist Centre. They climbed up six steps to reach the big, heavy wooden door, which was suddenly opened by a smiling old gentleman with white hair.

He greeted them saying 'Hello, my name is George. Hello newcomer, Mrs. Osbourne are you on tonight?'

'Yes, dear, I am.'

They walked downstairs to get a cup of tea, and placed a penny in the collection box. They walked upstairs after that. Heart and body warming up as they came to the Conan Doyle Hall. This was a big room, with a piano on the rostrum to the right, and row after row of chairs. Mrs. Osbourne told Charlie to have a seat anywhere he liked. He sat down by the door where they came in. She told him that the service would start in half an hour. Mrs. Osbourne walked out, and left the hall, and went downstairs to meditate and pray before the service.

'Hello Mimi'.

'Hello' said the other lady Medium.

'How's things?' asked Mrs. Osbourne.

'Oh fine' she replied.

'I have brought a new Medium. He will be very good one day. 'Are you coming up to see the service?' asked Mrs. Osbourne.

'No dear, I have Healing to do'.

'All right then, but I will introduce the young man to you later.'

'Oh, good! Have a nice evening.'

'Thank you, I am sure Spirit will be with me. They have never let me down so far. Bye bye now, I am going up, it's nearly time to begin'.

The Chairlady was already on the platform, seated in a very comfortable big brown chair, with arm rests. Next to her was another very large chair, which was for Mrs. Osbourne. The pianist climbed the two steps to the piano and sat down and started paying Chopin. All eyes were upon him, eagerly waiting for the arrival of the evening's Medium, Mrs. Osbourne. She entered swiftly, picking up her long brown skirt, swishing through the isle to get up to the platform as fast as she could.

The music ceased, and, after the applause died down, all fell silent. The air became vibrant and expectant. It was magically uplifting. The Chairlady rose to her feet, and begun to welcome everyone.

'Friends, it is nice to see the hall so full. I am sure Spirit will be with us tonight. God bless you all, and greetings to our Spirit friends. Can you stand up please, and we will sing the Healing song.'

Everyone stood up, and the pianist began to play for the congregation 'Gracious Spirit hear our anxious prayer!'.

When the song was finished all sat down as one. Mrs. Osbourne stood up and addressed the hall. 'My friends, I bring you greetings from the Spirit World, and I waste no Spirit Time at all by going directly to the messages. If I may begin with you dear, in the third row, to the left of the lady with the black dress and white shawl. Yes I come to you. Bless you! Your husband is with me, William, – Bill. He died very suddenly; he has suffered with the condition of gout on the large toe. He died with a sudden stroke condition. He brings love to you, and a pink rose. He is talking about Rosie and Paula.'

'Yes, I understand.'

'And Cillia or Cecillia.'

'Yes, she was my sister.'

'She is fine now – she died of a bowel condition – all her systems shut down, one by one.'

'Yes I understand.'

'Sends love to Joss this side. Yes, her husband is still here. Bobo, the terrier, is here with her.'

'Yes she did have that dog. The dog Bobo died of old age. Bobo turned 16 years and 7 months.

'Your sister is mentioning August as an anniversary'.

'Yes, it's her birthday.'

'Your father is here too. He died of a brain haemorrhage.'

'Yes, he did indeed die of that condition'.

'Who is Noel?'

'My brother-in-law.'

'Still to the earth plane. They withdraw the energy, and so I will leave you with their blessings, and undying love. God bless you!'

'And you too!'

'Winifred, is there someone here called Winifred?'

'Yes, that's me', both a lady and gentleman answered quickly.

The Medium said 'Only one of you is called Johns.'

'It is me', the lady answered. She was wearing a blue velvet dress.

'Yes, my dear, it is for you, indeed. Gwyn is here, and he talks about Wales. Yes, I understand he talks of Lombard Street.'

'Oh yes, he worked there.'

'He had thrombosis.'

'Yes, he did.'

'He sends all his love to you, and he gives you a November anniversary.'

'Yes, he died in November.'

'Just a minute, he was very ill by the 11th of November, but he died on the 18th of November.'

'Yes, he did indeed.'

'He talks about a sewing basket he gave you as a last present.'

'Yes that was his last present to me.'

'I understand very well. Thank you. And who is Lorenz?'

'My son here.'

'He sends his love to his son, and try to encourage him with his Law studies.'

'Oh yes, thank you!'

'He says his son will be a barrister in the Old Bailey.'

'I hope so. Thank you!'

'I leave you with that, and God be with you always, bless you!'

'Bless you, too!'

'Now I am coming to you sir, with the blue shirt and tie.'

'Thank you, bless you!'

'Your father was a textile merchant, he is talking to me now, and he was born in York. August he gives me, and October, as anniversaries. June linking with this side, and the name Annette, or rather Annie, yes, I can take that. Sheelagh, an aunty, is spirit, and sends her love to you too, and to your good wife and sons. George and Michael and Ben, on the other side.'

'Ben was our Alsatian – German Shepherd, cross-bred.'

'Yes, he has gone very recently.'
'Yes, 3 weeks ago to the day.'
'You had another dog – you called him King Lias.'
'Yes, I did.'
'He died of a sudden heart embolism.'
'Yes, he did just that.'
'His love is still with you, he says he loved you more than any other in your family, and he slept next to your bed, your side of the bed, no the right. He used to wake you up.'
'Yes he always did just that.'
'They all send their undivided love to you. They do come around in your sleep state.'
'Yes, I dreamt of them to be with them one more time, and running in golden meadows uphill.'
'You have really met up with them, not only dreamt of them. You were there, it was not a dream, but they did not want to frighten you.'
'I accept that, and thank you.'
'God bless you, and I leave you with that.'

Charlie just sat there with his mouth wide open. He was very excited, and thought I want to do that! I want people to seem happier to be reunited with lost loved ones once more. I have to do that, and I want to do it! If they want me to be a Medium I am willing to be one, and be a good and honest one too! I will stick to what the communicator is telling me carefully, and I will do my best under any kind of test to tell the truth, and at any cost. I am ready! Let the work begin now!

When he got home, Charlie went to the pantry. There wasn't any food, and the stove was very cold. The house was very quiet, as everyone was asleep. He went to the tap…oh well, water will do now. He drank eagerly to take away the hunger pangs, and turned around and went to the darkened bed chamber to sleep, to rest, to dream. I wonder who will come into my dreams tonight? He pulled the blanket over his head and begun to breathe heavily, and suddenly he was asleep. Or was he? A lady appeared.

'I am your other helper. My name is Leonora, you can call me Nora. I am the sister of Mary, and I will work with you always.' Nora smiled and told him 'I will see you again soon…very soon. Bless you for now, until we meet again, and meet we will.' Nora was gone.

When morning came it was cold and wet, and very, very windy. The raindrops fell heavily on the window pane. Another cold morning, Charlie thought. He washed his face in the water basin. The water was so very cold it hurt his face. Never mind, thought Charlie, I must get ready to go out. It was 5a.m., and it was still very dark outside and murky. A typically ghastly November morning. Charlie put his shoes on, and shut the front door behind him gently, so as not to wake anyone.

He was walking towards Fleet Street. It was pouring with rain and before too long Charlie's hair and face were wet, and, before too long, he was soaked through. Nevertheless he arrived and knocked on the door in front of him, and asked if there was any work today. The old man said that the only work available was the usual paper round. Charlie collected his papers and wrapped them with some brown paper to protect them from the rain, and got on with the task of delivering them from door to door. When he only had a few papers left he stood under a canopy and held up the last few copies to sell. Eventually he managed to sell the lot. He'd had a good day, and thought about the food he could buy. He walked to Covent Garden Market. It was nearly closing time, but he managed to get some potatoes and fish, wrapped up in some old newspaper. He carefully carried his precious packages home, and went straight to the pantry. The old stove was lit, and blazing away. Charlie laid the food carefully onto the table, and Charlotte exclaimed' Oh, my boy, we can have a real dinner tonight!'

'Yes we can', replied Charlie.

Charlotte began to peel the potatoes, they were half frozen, but they would have to do, she thought. She poured some oil into a pan, and put the fish and the potatoes in, ready to be cooked. 'A meal fit for a King' said Charlotte.

Charlie remained quiet as he'd been hungry all day. When the meal was ready, they hastily pulled the chairs to the table, and sat down. Eating with their fingers, it tasted better, and they had some watery tea to wash it down with. Charlie was so tired that after supper he went straight to bed. He turned down the lamp and went to bed, pulling the blanket up to his chin to keep warm. A few minutes past, or could it have been as long as an hour, a light filled the room, and it was so bright that Charlie thought it must be from Heaven above. Charlie looked up, and thought 'Oh, God, this is wonderful! Is anyone here? Who is present here?'

The familiar lady appeared with the light….the light faded away, and she started to shine out. It was Nora again. 'Oh what a big surprise' Charlie exclaimed!

'I told you I would come to you whenever you needed me, and so here I am. You are my charge while you live. I will protect your steps always. Do you believe me?'

'I do trust you, my lady.'

'Call me Nora' she said 'I will be always Nora to you.'

The morning came too soon again, and Charlie looked out of the window, 'Not bad, he thought, at least it wasn't raining. He still remembered last night's fish and chips, and how good they had tasted. The thought of them brought saliva to his mouth. He was hungry again. He washed his face. Same old routine again, thought Charlie, as he put on his shoes, and pulled his cape around him tightly, and slowly made his way to the front door, and closed it behind him. The morning air was cold, and it hit him, and the hunger pangs were getting worse. He was young and hungry. 'Oh dear God help me, I am so hungry.' He looked down and found a shilling. His eyes started to shine and then to ache as he felt the hot salty tears roll down his cold cheeks. 'Dear Lord, I sincerely thank you!' He walked on, thinking as soon as the cobbler opens, he would be able to get a pair of shoes, and he could also buy some food. He felt very rich indeed – one whole shilling! 'Oh, God is very good to me….it is a miracle what happened to me! One whole shilling and it's all mine! Wait until I tell Mrs. Osbourne this, and Charlotte, and all the family – Wow!!' Charlie thought.

He started to whistle now, and the bakery was just opening. He went in and bought a loaf of bread, and quickly unwrapped it from its paper. It was warm and smelt heavenly, and it tasted even better. He tore another piece off, and the hunger was melting away. What a wonderful day…what a wonderful…wonderful day he mused to himself….God is Great……Life is Great……..

He turned 19 years old, and Belgrave Square awaited him. He walked through the familiar door, and saw Mrs. Osbourne come towards him.

'Oh, Charlie, how are you?'

'How are you, dear lady?'

'I'm fine indeed, but you have grown, dear boy. You are a man now!' Mrs. Osbourne noticed that Charlie had grown a moustache.

'Oh, yes, I suppose I have. I want to be a Medium like you Lady Osbourne. I see them, and I hear them, they are all around me.'

'I know boy, I know. Well now, you can sit with me here. I have just started a circle for people like you.'

'Really?'

'Oh yes, it is a bit new, but we can teach you to reach out towards the Spirit People. The Movement needs you. You will learn our Seven Principles and Code of Conduct. How to sit properly, and to serve the Spirit well. No half measures, my son. Do you understand that? You must learn to give it your all. You will be able to do that well.'

'Like you?' Charlie asked.
'Yes I suppose like me, or even better, Charlie.'
'Oh, Lady Osbourne, you have made me very happy indeed!'
'That's good. We start tonight at 8 p.m.'
'Oh, that is wonderful!'

8p.m. could not come quick enough for Charlie. He was very eager, and more than just willing to get on with it.

When 8 p.m. arrived all six of them settled down. There was Melanie, Geoffrey, Katrina, Stephanie and, of course, Charlie. There are more ladies than men, Charlie thought. Mrs. Osbourne settled down with them, and they formed a full circle. The air was filled with expectancy, a bit like a pregnant lady with child. They turned the flame of the lamps down very low, then Mrs. Osbourne pointed to the middle of the circle, where there was a vase filled with roses. She told them to look at the beauty of the roses, take it in, and then she told them to close their eyes. She told them to leave the earthly life behind them, and, taking deep breaths, to let the Spirit come to them. 'Send loving thoughts towards your helpers, and speak when you are impressed. Meditation will now begin' she said.

All fell very silent; no shuffling of feet could be heard, except the slow deliberate breathing of the souls gathered together in God's name. Some time had passed, and it was Geoffrey who started to talk. Slowly at first, as if he were tongue tied. His eyes were shut very firmly, and he had a stern expression on his face. It was changing, transfiguring, and then resembled a very old man with Mongolian features.

'I am your Guide' the voice spoke very slowly at first. 'My name is Khan, Dr Khan. I am here to help all of you and to bring you the greetings of the World of Spirit; I am also the Guide who is designated to you. All of you here tonight watch carefully. Open your eyes to see. My face will be changing to resemble your lost loved ones. Do you understand me?'

'Yes, we do', everyone replied quietly.

Charlie's eyes nearly fell out of their sockets. He saw his brother, Nicky's, face at first, who had died when he was less than two years old. 'I am here, brother'. Charlie nearly fell off his chair. 'Greetings to you!'

'Thank you!' Charlie said 'Bless you!'

Then suddenly an old lady appeared on Geoffrey's face, surrounded with a floaty white substance – ectoplasm. The lady wore a broach shaped like an oval locket where she kept a strand of hair. 'Evelyn is my name' she said slowly materialising, with her hair in a bun. She wore a brown dress, with a white collar up to the chin, which was buttoned up very tightly. 'I was a teacher. I taught young children before they went to school. I was a governess in Brighton. Greetings my child, I say to you, Melanie. I am your great grandmother. Do you recognise me?'

'Yes I have heard of you, and yes, I do' Melanie replied.

'I have brought Charles with me too, and Arthur, your grandfather. They all send their love to you. Aunt Emily had a parrot called Coco, who is with her.'

'Yes, I know about the Coco bird, thank you', said Melanie.

'Coco was her name, even so, it was a he, but nobody has known that. He talked a lot.'

'Yes I have been told that.'

'I leave you now, and God bless you child', and she left.

The face changed again into a gentleman's face, with a large moustache. He was wearing a grey flannel suit, and a bowler hat, and walking stick. 'I am Harold, and I come to my niece here, Katherina.'

'Thank you, thank you, dear uncle, it is you, isn't it?'

'Of course it is me, were you expecting someone else?'

'How is my father?'

'He is with me, my dear.'

'Thank you, uncle. How is Tom, my son, uncle?'

'He is with us in the higher Life. He is attending spirit school. His lungs are perfect now, and he is well.'

'Oh thank God, thank you, thank you', she sobbed with relief.

'Well, my dear, people come and people go….let go…. We all survive this life. I am as real as I ever was. Look at me now, do I not look well?'

'Yes, uncle, you do!'

'All is well little one! I must go now. I can't hog the limelight. I love you, dear. I love you and bless you. My love to your mother, Veronica, as well as Stephanie.'

'I will let them know you are all well in the Spirit World, uncle.'

'Bless you now – bless you child….' the voice faded away to make room for someone else.

Geoffrey's face changed once more. This time it resembled a little lady with horn-rimmed rounded glasses 'My name is Eloisa, and I come to greet you all, dear friends. I greet you Stephanie, my darling.'

'Who are you?' asked Stephanie 'Do I know you?'

'I am your aunty, my dear. My liver failed, my love, and I now let you know that I am well, and fit again.

'Oh aunty, I never knew you, but I welcome you.'

'Thank you my dear. I come to bring you light into your life, and love from all who have gone before you. Winifred is with me, and Moira.'

'Bless you aunty! Thank you for coming.'

'I have to go now. God be with you!'

For Stephanie contact with her grandmother seemed to go too quickly. It was Charlie's turn, or was it?

Geoffrey's face changed again to an Indian gentleman. 'Oh my god' thought Charlie, I've seen this face before, in my dreams.

'It was no dream. I come to see you Charlie. I am your guide and you recognised me', he spoke slowly.

'Yes I do, I do indeed. Thank you for coming!'

'I come to let you know that you will be a shining light, a

torch for humanity. You will be a great instrument for spirit in your world. Many people will come to see you, and you will give solace to all! You will dry their tears, and you will let them all know life has no ends, only new beginnings – transformation only, do not call it death. Do not fear the passing, and tell others the same. We all survive. Where I come from your kind live on. This is the world of spirit, where all knowledge is known, and where all is available to those who seek the truth. The great message lives on, where Percival lives, and the place I call home. I am on the seventh level. It does not mean much to you yet, but you will understand all that later on. It will be strife and suffering in your world, and the time will come when you will be needed the most. You will only understand all this later, when you have passed your earthly age of thirty, and you will see your world transforming, not for the best, as I can see it. There will be much suffering and war will be coming, because of Man's great greed, and hatred will come to your world. By 1933–44 you will see terrible power rising, and it will destroy many. Brother will rise against brother, but the world will survive. You will survive to teach others how to live a better life. You will be a new teacher for that new world, which will be born after the ashes have blown away.'

Charlie listened very carefully. He did not like what he heard but kept it to himself. 'I understand what you tell me, and your talk of Great War, which I do not understand yet, but I believe you.'

'Charlie, my boy, I will never leave you. I am with you always, to help. Many people will seek you out in their hundreds. Make preparations for the work ahead of you. You will not do it all alone. Do not be afraid, I stand by you always. You will be a good man Charlie, and my medium. Thank you.'

'No, thank you' said Charlie.

'Yours will not be an easy road, but you will be looked after all the way, so do not fret. I am always at your left side. You can talk to me and you will hear my voice in your ear. You will know that I am always near. Call me when you need me. You will not be exempt from suffering in your world, but I promise your needs shall be met. Ask, and you shall get help for yourself, as much as for all other souls seeking your undivided help. I leave you with that, Charlie, for now, but remember that I am never far away. Send your thoughts to me, and I will be there.'

'Thank you' whispered Charlie. His mouth was dry, and he was gasping for breath now. 'What a responsibility, indeed, yes it is', he thought. The Indian left as quickly as he had appeared, and a very tired looking Geoffrey sighed, and reached down for a glass of water, which was under his seat.

Mrs. Osbourne turned to the circle and said 'Well my friends, tonight's session is coming to a close, but before we close this lovely circle, I would like to pray that Light and Love go with you all, when we part and go our separate ways. Bless you all, and we also thank our spirit friends, who have made their spirit return. Goodnight all, and do not forget next Monday we will meet here at 8p.m.'

'No we won't', everyone replied.

'Goodnight, Mrs. Osbourne' said Charlie, as he left the room. He inhaled the good fresh night air. He was breathing deeply and was very moved by the night's experience. He started to walk faster, and, as he passed a beggar, he apologised to him, for he had no money to spare him, but Charlie thought 'tomorrow is another day'.

He quickened his pace, as he would have a very long walk home if he missed the bus that would take him to Mansel Street. When the bus arrived, he got on, and promptly fell asleep. He was very tired. As the bus approached Aldgate he suddenly woke up. He had a feeling it had been his guide who had gripped his shoulders, and thanked him for waking him up just in time. As he put his hands into his pockets he felt some pennies left. 'Oh, no work tomorrow', he thought, and jumped off the bus, and headed straight home.

Mary Ann looked Charlie in the eyes, 'My son, you seem happy tonight.'

'I am, dear mother, I am happy!'

'Really?' Mary Ann asked.

'Yes, so many wonderful things happened tonight.'

'Where have you been, boy?'

'I was in heaven!'

'Heaven?'

'Yes mother, or at least very near to it.'

'You must tell me all about it, son.'

'Mother dear, I'm not sure if you would understand it.'

'Well son, you can try, can't you?'

'Yes I suppose' his tongue appeared stuck as he tried to get the words out 'I went to a séance.'

'Séance?'

'Yes, it was wonderful, and my spirit has been lifted!'

'Indeed son, indeed. So?'

'So, mother, let me get my breath back, and I will tell you. I saw…I heard miracles happen.'

'I believe in God son, so don't be shy. Do talk about it. Will you now?'

'All right. It all started when I met Lady Osbourne.'

'Who is she?'

'A medium, mother, a medium. A lady who gives spirit messages from dead people.'

'Oh, my Lord, is she sane?'

'As sane as you or I mother.'

'Are you sure, son?'

'Yes I have seen her working. I have seen dead people materialising on someone's face, when I sat in that circle. I have seen my Guide Mother. I'll never be alone….I see them.'

'How often?' she asked.

'Well, come to think about it now, very often when I go to

sleep, or when I am able to relax. I hear the dead speak to me.'

'Well that is wonderful, Charlie. I would like to go with you to see Lady Osbourne, and you told me about Mini as well.'

'Yes I did, and they are wonderful people, and they are doing wonderful things. They seem so ordinary, but so disciplined.'

'Well, boy, that is good. When is your next meeting?'

'Next week', Charlie said. 'I can't wait to get back there. It seems so wonderful and somehow so natural too. I will take you there mother, but you can't come to the circle with me.'

'Why on earth not, son?'

'Because it is a closed circle, and only the developing mediums are allowed there. I'm sorry.'

'I understand Charlie. Well I am happy for you. That makes one happy doesn't it?'

'Yes it does Mother to see the things I can see you can't even begin to understand it.'

'I would love to see what you see Charlie, but if I can't, take me along there, anyway.'

'I will Mother. I promise you.'

The days rolled by, along with the weeks and seasons, and in no time at all it was 1933. In Germany many changes started to take place. Hitler became Chancellor and started to gather strength and power. Many had read his book *Mein Kampf*, and a great many people followed him, and were mesmerised by all he said and did.

Charlie was thirty-three years old. By now he had left his old house, and had moved to Willesden Lane, in Kilburn. He was happier now, and had grown into a bright, strapping man, and despite the Depression lingering, he always had a smile on his face. His mother had passed away in St Mary's Hospital, Paddington. He had been told that she had cancer in the abdomen, and they couldn't operate, as the cancer had spread throughout her body. When Charlie looked back and remembered her, the tears welled up in his blue eyes, and he felt very sad, as the hurt of losing her had been so very deep. He had taken his mother to the spiritualist meetings a few times, and she had been so very happy there. She did have the best survival evidence given to her time and time again. That was the time when she felt really good about life, as if she could fly. Leaving the meetings with a sense of having been uplifted, and looking up to Charlie, she felt so proud of her son, the Medium. He was tall, and she shrank in stature towards the end of her life, having to endure such pain, that was caused by the cancer. Charlie remembered the young woman she used to be, able to handle just about anything, even the hard times. She had been the driving force behind him, always, and she was the one that always kept him going. Dear old Charlotte passed away to spirit in 1931. Her husband, George, had gone before her, but had not suffered as she had done. His death had been sudden, as he had had a massive coronary.

Charlie walked toward the old cemetery in Willesden Lane, where they had both been buried. He knew he was only visiting their memory there, as they lived on. How well he knew that. 'The earthly remains are here, but they are not. No point in coming here', he thought to himself, 'I'll go home now and send my love to them, yes, I will send all my love to them, and light a candle for them.' That was the way of the world. People came and people went, all just passing through.

He stopped outside 76 Willesden Lane, and opened the red ugly door, to climb to the third floor, where he lived. He thought 'I am nearer to God at the top.' He took the steps two at a time, wanting to get into his rented room fast. Not that it was a wonderful place to live in, but it was better than nothing. There was an old army bed in the room, along with a creaky old wardrobe in one corner – not that he had many clothes to put into it. He did have a great many books, which he loved, including works by Shakespeare, Dickens and the Bronte sisters. He also loved music, and amongst his favourite composers were Chopin and

Bach. Music is good for the soul, but Charlie had no gramophone player. 'Well, one day I will buy one', he often thought to himself. By now he had become a fully fledged Medium and Healer. He needed a telephone as well, but like most things in his life, a telephone would also have to wait, as he couldn't afford one.

The landlady's loud voice interrupted his thoughts, followed by a heavy knock on his door. 'Mr Charlie, phone call for you, come downstairs' she bellowed. Charlie made his way down the stairs and towards the phone.

'Mr. Charles?' a voice asked on the other end.

'Yes' Charlie answered.

'We want you to come to Bristol tomorrow, to our church. Can you come?'

'Yes, I am free tomorrow'.

'We need you for our Sunday service, so we can count on you?'

'Yes, as always' replied Charlie.

Charlie got up at 6 a.m., the following morning, to catch the train from Paddington, which would take him to Bristol. When he arrived at the station he waited for the announcement on the loudspeaker that would tell him which platform to head for. Platform 4, and he made his way towards the train, and settled down on a seat nearest the window. As the train pulled out of the station he unpacked his breakfast of bread and dripping, and ate it heartily. He would have some tea when he arrived, and having finished his meal, he closed his eyes, relaxed, and fell asleep for the rest of the journey. When the train arrived in Bristol he made his way out of the station, and turned left, then right, and found himself outside a house with the sign 'Spiritualist Assembly', and he knew he had arrived at the correct address. He made his way to the front door, but as this was shut, he made his way around to the back of the house, and knocked on the door. A friendly-faced woman opened the door, and greeted him

'Come in, you must be Mr. Charles'.

'Yes, I am'.

'Bless you for coming all this way!'

'Yes, indeed it is a long way, but I will travel any distance where I am called to give the message to all. There is no death. There is no death victory but Spirit World gain when one is passed to the higher life!'

Once he had received refreshment, the service went very well. On the platform there was some water for him. Mediumship was very thirsty work! He was introduced to the congregation as Mr. Charles. He noticed the people's reaction when they smiled. They had heard of his work. Good mediums were making headlines in the Press as well as the bad ones, but who is to Judge? Judge not! He was good, and Charlie was probably aware of that. Even so, he never showed off. During the service he went to the back of the Church pointing to a young lady. 'My dear I am coming to you. I believe Cecilia is your name.'

'Yes that is my name.'

'I have been told that by Joe, your lovely father, who died of blood disorders. A clot in the leg, and his leg had to be amputated, but despite their efforts, the clot made its way to his heart, and he went instantly. Your father says that he had emphysema as well, which affects the breathing. He is telling me you paint well, using oils.'

'Yes, I do!' she exclaimed.

'He also says that you have a brother, who is with you tonight.'

'Yes, he is here tonight, sitting in the third row from the front.'

'Your father died in October, and his birthday was in June. An anniversary is coming up.'

'Yes, I understand' she said.

'He says the name MacArthur means something to you.'

'Yes, it does indeed. He worked for my father.'

'He has joined him in the Higher Life now, and they have met up.'

'Oh good!' she replied.

The Service ended, and everyone thanked Charlie, and said it had been an uplifting experience for all. Charlie headed for the station, and a gruelling journey back to London lay ahead of him, but this was of no importance to him. He started his journey back to London on the last train out of Bristol, which left at 11.30 p.m. He slept for most of the journey.

When morning came he felt very good, despite the awful tasting coffee he had to drink. He flew down the flight of stairs in the building where he lived as he set off for work. He was a clerk now in the newspaper office, hoping one day he would become a journalist. 'I can do it', he thought and he did. Despite the promotion, his wage packet remained meagre. 3 shillings and 6 pence, not much, but it would have to do. His rent came to 3 shillings a month, but he could just about afford to live.

He sat down by his desk, and had a good look at the news. It was 1940, and Britain was at war with Germany. He started to type his report, which would appear in the following day's edition. It was winter, and it was very cold! He blew into his hands to try to keep them warm. The miners were on strike, and so the supply of coal was getting smaller and smaller, and London was suffering terribly. When he finished his day's work, he headed for the bus which would take him to Belgrave Square. Getting ready for the service mentally on the draughty bus was quite hard, but he prayed for his Guides to be with him during the night's service.

When he arrived the place was filled with people with expectant faces and hearts. He took his seat on the rostrum, and relaxed into the big brown chair 'which was fit for a King' Charlie thought. He was introduced by the ChairLady, who rose to her feet saying 'Tonight we welcome Mr Charles, our Medium for tonight's service.'

Charlie got up, and started to welcome friends. 'I need a few moments, then I will know who I am with'. He started to pace the platform, and began 'I come to the lady in the red dress. Yes, my dear, you. Jane, in the world of spirit, comes to greet you.'

'She is my sister.'

Charlie continued 'Your father is with me now, Bernard, and the bulldog is with him.'

The lady in red explained that the dog had been with them since she was a little girl.

'He is talking about a large family of eleven.'

'Yes, we were eleven children.'

'He says seven are with him now.'

'Yes, he is right, they are' she replied.

'Only four of you are left here.'

'That is so.'

'Who had the budgie?'

'My uncle, Charles.'

'Charles is here, and bringing your mother, his sister, with him. Saying Goldie is with me.'

'Oh that is our golden Labrador dog. I grew up with him.'

'Your mother is saying Goldie lived until she was 16 – a ripe old age.'

'Yes he did. Yes I remember him.'

'I leave you with all their love, my dear lady.'

'Thank you. Thank you, and bless you!'

'Now I come to you sir', pointing to a bald headed gentleman, near to the back row.

'Yes' said the man, acknowledging Charlie. 'Thank you for coming to me.'

Charlie smiled 'It is the spirits who guided me to you. A naval officer sends love to you, and mentions May and August as anniversaries.'

'My father was in the Navy.'

'He says he was born in Plymouth, and so were you.'

'Yes, he was, and so was I.'

'You lost your hair, due to financial worries, otherwise you are very healthy.'

'Yes sir', he replied to Charlie. 'I lost everything, except my sense of humour. That is all I have left.'

'Not exactly, your father is saying you have got your home, and your wife is a lovely lady, Mary, and your lovely girl is growing up.'

'I suppose I have to be thankful for that', he said.

'Your father is saying you will restart your business again, and help will be given to you.'

'Bless you, and thank you!'

'Bless you too, sir' said Charlie.

'I come to you, now' said Charlie, pointing to a petite lady, with blonde hair, who was dressed in white.

'Thank you', she replied shyly.

'Your brother, Andrew, is here, and your grandmother, Sally, is here too. Your brother took his own life.'

'Oh yes, he did.'

'He is very sorry now for what he did, and he now knows it was wrong to do. Your grandmother, Ada, is also here.'

'Oh, my father's mother. I didn't know him very well.'

'He knows you, and he has watched you growing up. You have problems with your foot.'

'Yes, I have.'

'You also have a problem with your breathing.'

'Yes, I do.'

'They are withdrawing their energy, so I will leave you with that.'

'I come to you', Charlie said, pointing to a lady sitting near the front, 'yes, you dear, wearing the blue blouse.'

'Thank you!'

'I see a naval base, and a gentleman 5'.10" tall, teaching them to be officers and gentlemen.'

'Oh my god, he is my father, Thomas!'

'Who is Peter? He talks about Peter, and sends his love to

him.'

'He is my brother.'

'He says he has a fantastic voice for opera, and that he will be a singer.'

'That is all is wants to do', she replied.

'He is saying that he will help him. Who had the injury to the hand?'

'Someone worked in the printers, the machine came down on his fingers, on the left hand.'

'Yes, he says he was lucky, it could have been the right hand!'

'Yes, I suppose so.'

'He says he smoked, and he was tired, so when he pulled down the press he forgot his fingers were there. He loved a cigarette! He then just went to bed, and died in his sleep.'

'Yes, he did.'

'He enjoyed his funeral, and he is saying it was very nice to see so many people attended it.'

'Yes, they did.'

'What is the link with South Africa?'

'My cousin is there.'

'He talks about Kenya, and you were there, too.'

'Yes, I have lived there for many happy years.'

'Home is here for you now, he says.'

'Yes, I think so.'

'You have a lovely son.'

'Yes, I do.'

'You have a daughter as well, and her name is Amelia.'

'Yes, that is her name.'

'God bless you now, and I leave you with their blessings.'

The night service came to a close, and he sat down, only to rise up again, saying 'Bless you all, and remember that when we depart from tonight's service your loved ones will be with you always.'

The next day he returned to Belgrave Square and met

Nicholas, who was waiting for him. He was a psychic artist.
'Hello my dear old chap.'
'Hello' said Charlie.
'When will we get together to work here?'
'Next month', replied Charlie. 'I recommended you because of your brilliant drawing, and your ability to capture the spirit portrait. Can I say something?', continued Charlie.
'Yes ,do'.
'Well, you draw using charcoal. We need to see colour.'
'I can do that. Would it be better?'
'I think so. People do recognise people done in black and white, but life is full of colours and nothing is black and white, even though we do have grey areas in life.'
'Yes I suppose so. I will bring the easel and large white sheets of paper and coloured pencils.'
'Great!' exclaimed Charlie. 'You will see the difference.'
'I suppose we will. Well, old chap, I'll see you next month on the platform here. I'm looking forward to that', said Nicholas.
'See you, then.'
They said their goodbyes, and headed home. Nicholas lived in Greenwich, also in a bed-sit, and worked as a carpenter to keep a roof over his head. 'It's a living of sorts', he thought to himself. 'I do my best, and the spirit will do the rest.'
A month passed by, and the evening arrived. The hall was full to the brim, and the air was filled with great expectation. They climbed onto the platform. Nicholas got ready by putting up the easel and paper, and arranging his coloured pencils. The chairman took his seat for the evening, along with Charlie, and the pianist began to play. They all started to sing "Gracious Spirit". When they finished everyone sat down, and Charlie stood up, and said 'Allow me to introduce to you our psychic artist, whose name is Nicholas'. Nicholas did not waste any time, and began to draw the image of a little boy, aged around six years old. As the face started forming ,Charlie said 'Essex, there is a link with

Essex and Benji.'

An elderly lady in the first row answered. 'That was my son'. She continued to look at the drawing, and could see his curly hair and the blue of his eyes, as blue as the sky. A cat was drawn next to him.

'She is Mimi', said Charlie.

'Oh yes, we did have that cat' and a teddy bear was drawn. 'Oh, he did have this teddy bear when he was little, and he kept it close by his side all the time.'

'He drowned whilst trying to learn to swim. The current had pulled him under, and I am getting Norfolk', said Charlie.

'Yes, it happened there.'

'Thank you, and God be with you!'

The next one was an elderly man, and he had dark eyes, and semi-dark mid brown hair, and a much wrinkled face, with a sombre expression. Charlie started talking. 'He was in the Army, the 1st World War. He had a wound to the head, and no surgeon could help him. The wound became septic, and he died in the trenches.'

A gentleman replied, slowly at first. His voice coming from towards the entrance door. 'He was my uncle.'

'He says he was born in Bispham, near Blackpool.'

'Yes, he was', the man replied.

'He says he comes from a family of five.'

'Yes, he did.'

'Your mother, Louise, was his sister.'

'Yes, she was.'

'Your mother is with him now. And you have a daughter, Lorraine.'

'Yes, I have indeed!'

The picture was finished, carefully rolled up, and handed over to the gentleman, who said 'Oh, it means a lot to me! Thank you!'

The next drawing was of a lady, who had a strong face, slim

features, and high check bones, with semi-blonde hair, and in her forties.

'Her name is Eilene' said Charlie 'She died of lung and breast cancer. She is giving me Clapham.'

A lady replied from the back of the hall 'She was my grandmother.'

'She taught in the local school in Clapham. She was a schoolteacher there. She died aged 41, never reaching her 42nd birthday.'

'Thank you so much!'

'And now what have we got here?' Charlie looked at the St. Bernard dog, who appeared on the right of the picture 'He is Bertie, but wait a minute', a gentleman appeared in the picture who had a young proud face. 'Ian, yes it is Ian, he is telling me that he comes from Kent. He died at the age of twenty-four, the name of Primrose comes with him, and a Lillian on this side.'

'I am Lillian', a lady raised her hand, 'I am his sister.'

'He died on his motorcycle. He got thrown from it. It was dark and late at night', added Charlie.

'Yes, it was.'

'Who comes from Fulham Palace Road?' asked Charlie.

'I do.'

'You have three small children?'

'Yes, I have.'

'You carry with you something belonging to him.'

'Yes I do a flask. I carry some water with me in it.'

'It is a silver flask.'

'Yes, it is.'

'He is saying he never used this flask, as he was not a drinker.'

'No, he was not. You are correct!'

'He never understood why you bought him that flask for Christmas, as a present.'

'Well, I liked that flask, and I did not know what else to buy for him.'

'He was in the Cavalry.'

'Yes, he was!'

'A very proud soul, eager to rise beyond his level in society. He did try.'

'Yes, he did.'

'He is a lovely soul.'

'Yes, he was.'

'He still is. Love never ever dies, it goes on, and the only link between our two worlds is love only' Charlie added.

'Thank you!' she said, and gratefully accepted the rolled-up portrait.

The chairman rose to his feet, and said 'Well that is all for tonight, and thank you all for coming, and the light be with you all, and show you the way! Goodnight.'

The year now was 1944. The bombs and doodlebugs filled the London air. Charlie looked out from the darkened rooms, due to the blackout curtains. 'Well they are coming again', he thought. The sky was heavy with all the noise that the bombs made. The planes kept coming, and each time he had to go to the basement with the other tenants for safety. A small candle burned, and Charlie told the frightened people that they would all survive, and they had to keep their spirits up. He heard the planes cross over again, but they had a different sound to them. It was the R.A.F., and Charlie, like everyone else, knew that they would do all they could.

'Sure will', Molly said, who was a shop assistant in her thirties.

'It will be over soon', Charlie was saying.

'All that rationing, I've hardly any coupons left, and only two eggs a week' she said.

'Never mind, we will overcome this', Charlie said.

In that basement, in the middle of the Blitz, a stove was lit, and a large saucepan was placed on it. Molly got up and started to stir the soup, which contained a few vegetables....more water than vegetables. But at least they would not starve, and besides it was warm, and when they had finished they felt better. Some even left the shelter of the basement, even though the raid had not finished. 'Tomorrow is another day', Charlie thought.

As morning arrived they all went back upstairs, and found that the attic of the building was completely destroyed. There was just a great big hole left! Charlie set about finding some materials in the rubble which he could use to fix the hole. The glass windows had all been shattered. Charlie went to the local wood yard to see if he could find some wood to repair the frames, even though he had no glass to put in them. He was happy when he'd finished, and as happy as he was ever going to be with a war on. Many people had been left homeless, fires burned all over the place, but they all helped one another. Tom lived on the first floor in Charlie's building. Charlie knocked on his door.

'Who is it?'

'It's me, Charlie.'

Tom opened the door, and told Charlie that he had an aunty in Hook, Hampshire. 'We can go there. Would you like to come with me?'

'Good idea' said Charlie.

'I've got a bike, and it will take a while to get there, but we'll get there somehow. It's safer in the countryside.'

'I bet', Charlie said.

'A lot of people have been evacuated already.'

'Well it will soon be over', Charlie said.

'Not yet' said Tom. 'And while we're there, we can do some work.'

'Such as?' Charlie asked.

'Helping out on the land.'

'Food', thought Charlie, and already he felt better. Even the thought of food made Charlie feel better!

The following morning they both set off for Hampshire. It was a very long and slow journey, with the planes above them and chaos below. Despite this, the sky was lovely with billowing clouds, and Charlie thought 'Not all is lost yet!'. Tom believed the very same, although not in the same way, because he wasn't a Psychic Medium. Tom was British through and through, and was a patriot of his country, and he believed that the British would have the victory, and eventually the war was all over.

There were huge celebrations on D-Day. It was 1945, and everywhere people were running to the streets and hugging each other, and smiling. Conditions did not improve overnight, but the rebuilding began. Everybody pulled together, and the sale of utility furniture in the Army & Navy stores helped. Utility clothing, making do with whatever they could get hold of, was commonplace.

People started planning little gardens, but they had learnt, during the war, that a plot became something bigger, when people could grow their own vegetables on communal allotments. Charlie went to the back garden and dug up the lot. It was only 40 feet long, but he could grow a great deal of things on this plot of land. He had found some cabbage and carrot seeds, then planted them. It was Spring, and, by late summer, August, he'd be enjoying his hard work. He was also given a tomato plant, which he planted. He had a good selection of vegetables planted, and he hoped he would reap the rewards of his hard work. The war was indeed over, but things were slow to improve. Rationing books were still being used, and meat and eggs were difficult to get right up until 1947.

Charlie was now 47 years old. The time had passed quickly, maybe too quickly, as he had no wife or children, and Tom was also growing older.

He had been invited to Stanstead Hall, and Charlie was wondering how he was going to get there. Old Harry had a bike and cycle; in fact Harry had all kinds of vehicles next to his garage in Willesden Green. Charlie decided to walk to Harry's, and, as he got to his door, the smell of oil and petrol was overpowering.

'Hello, Harry!'
'Hello, old chap' said Harry.
'Harry, I'm in trouble!'
'What sort, Charlie?'
'Well I need a vehicle to get me to Stanstead Hall. I've been invited there to teach, and I haven't got a car.'
'I've got an old banger over there, the blue one' suggested Harry.
'That will do' exclaimed Charlie 'Can I borrow it?'
'Yes, you can have it for a week, if you like. I won't charge you for it.'
'That's very kind of you!' said Charlie.
'It's a Morris Minor, and it's a good car. It'll get you there and back.'
'Thank you so much! Thank you!' said Charlie. 'I'm really grateful.'

Charlie set off towards Stanstead. It was a rather bumpy ride, but he arrived safely. Essex wasn't that far, and it took him just an hour and a half, travelling at 30 miles an hour. The Great Hall was magnificent. It was an impressive building, surrounded by land stretching as far as the eye could see. Arthur Findlay, the famous spiritualist writer, had left the Hall and land to the Spiritualist Movement, and Charlie thought what a kind thing to do.

The place was full of beautiful wooden floors and carpet here and there. There was a sweeping staircase leading to the first floor, with a library on the ground and first floors. These were full of wonderful books; some were first editions, and some of them very old. Charlie could see that the condition of some were flaky and looked very delicate. Charlie was ushered to the first floor by the President of the college, and led to Arthur Findlay's room.

This room was really something! The large four poster bed took up most of the room, and a huge brown wardrobe with a washing table and water on it with a glass for drinking. He tested the bed, hard but good. He then looked out of the large bay window, which overlooked the grounds, and saw a wonderful tulip tree, and beyond that, many other trees of all shapes and sizes, in all different stages of growth. Under the trees he could see the well-kept canopy of green grass. He saw two cats, one stretching his front legs and looking very content, the other was patrolling the grounds. Charlie heard the voice of a lady call one of the cats 'Salmon', and watched as the black cat with white 'socks' moved towards the back door, where a plate of food was waiting for him. 'This is a real sanctuary' Charlie thought, and said out loud 'what a wonderful place this is!'

Suddenly a bell sounded, or was it a gong? All the guests were being summoned to dinner. Charlie made his way downstairs and into the great hall, where people were sitting around five large tables. At each table sat seven guests. The dinner arrived, and was served by the maids of the hall, who became waitresses at meal times. The first course was a non-descript soup that looked as if it had lentils in it, but Charlie wasn't sure. The second course arrived, and turned out to be bangers and mash, followed by Spotted Dick, and washed down with a glass of water. Charlie made his way to bed after all that.

The night started off as any other night. He had drawn the dark blue curtains, and went to bed. Two steps up to the king-sized bed. 'I could sleep here 'till eternity' Charlie thought, pulling up the lovely duvet, which was filled with warm feathers. What a joy this duvet was, so warm and light. Charlie was used to the heavy course blankets. 'I will sleep well here', Charlie mused.

At about 2 a.m. Charlie suddenly became aware that he was not alone in his room. A lady wearing a night cap was walking to the window, pacing up and down. Charlie sat bolt upright in bed, and watched her swishing long skirt as if it were brushing the wooden floor, but there was no sound! All was so very quiet and eerie. Charlie spoke 'What are you doing here? Who are you?' The lady smiled at him, and promptly faded away.

He couldn't wait until morning to ask the President of the College if he knew who the lady in his room, was. 'Oh, that was Mrs. Findley' he said to Charlie. 'She is always walking around you see. She loved that place, and she still comes here quite often. Others have seen here before.'

'Well, what an honour!' Charlie said. It was quite something!

'There are some other people here' said the President. 'There is a man with a bad leg, and he walks with a walking stick. Sometimes he drops it at people's doors'.

'I've only seen Mrs. Findley', Charlie said. 'She's a lovely lady, but she didn't speak to me.'

They sat down for their morning tea in the dining area. Everyone was so excited with the thought of what the day might hold for them, and all the students were chatting happily, following their good night's rest. The President got up and smiled at everyone. 'Good morning all. Today's classes are written down on a blackboard outside in the great hall. After breakfast please read the board to see where your classes will be held. Take care to go to the right place, and please note that doors will be locked, so do not be late, as this will upset the equilibrium and the atmosphere for you all. I sincerely hope that you all understand that. Thank you for your attention, and now please enjoy the day.'

The breakfast was soon over. 'Quite a few students', Charlie thought, 'and all wanting to be Mediums. We need all good souls for the work. In the end out of seventy perhaps two will make the grade. Ignorance is bliss. They are not aware of that yet, whatever happens to them, they will learn to be better people. That is good and serving the purpose in God's plan for us.'

He followed the crowd, and turned towards the downstairs library. He closed some of the windows, and pulled the heavy green velvet curtains with gold tasselled edges together. He went up to the platform, and poured a glass of water for himself, and placed it on the small round oak table, and sat down on the round Victorian padded chair, which, he thought, was very comfortable. He drank some of the water, cleansing his mind and body as he drank, and closed his eyes, sitting quietly and meditating, drawing his guides to be near his aura; his energy field.

The students started to come into the room, and took their respective seats. All the chairs were very comfortable, and, as they were going to be spending a long time in the room, it was important that the chairs be comfortable. All eyes were on Charlie. He started to open his eyes slowly, and took another gulp of water. 'I know you Frank', Charlie said, pointing to the first row of gathered students. 'You have been to another class of mine', Charlie continued.

'Yes', said Frank.

'Now please get up, and we will arrange the chairs in a double circle', said Charlie.

The students got up, and started to move the chairs around, to create the double circle. When they had finished, they moved the remaining chairs to the back of the room, and piled them on top of one another neatly. They sat down, and turning to them, Charlie said 'We will begin with a prayer. Great Father, Mother of God, we ask that the white light surround us, and that we will prosper in knowledge under Thy wings! We also invite our guides and helpers to attend with us, to guide us and help us to reunite us with our loved ones. Amen! Now we are going into the silence, and I want you to take deep breaths. Keep breathing quietly now, and focus your thoughts upward, leaving everything here behind. Close your eyes and visualise a beautiful waterfall. We are standing nearby. You feel the drops of water on your face. It is warm and comfortable, and you are a part of nature. Love, light and truth are yours. Be part of that now. Listen with your heart… something will happen soon. Go deeper into your own soul, and ask for the help of your own individual helpers consigned to you. Listen to the silence and go deeper'.

All sat with their eyes closed, and nothing stirred. Half an hour passed, and Charlie kept watching them, slowly turning his head in all directions.

'Open your eyes very slowly', he instructed them, 'and retain the information until it is your time to speak.' Charlie turned to the girl next to him, and said 'young lady, did you get something?'

'Yes, I have a message for Claire, the third one from me.'

Charlie quietly thanked her so as not to disturb the tranquillity of the room, as the circle was working as one. 'Well?', said Charlie, prompting the girl.

'I see a gentleman standing beside you.'

'Describe him', said Charlie.

'He is 5'. 9", and he has brown hair, and he is clutching his chest.'

'Yes, my father died from heart failure', said Claire.

'His name is Jonathan, and he is saying....'

'Go on', said Charlie, 'get more information'.

'Saying Ambrose nectar' she laughed, 'yes, he liked a drink or two. Talking about "The Anchor."

'It was a pub where we lived. He used to go there a lot.'

'He sends his love to Felicity, your mother.'

'Yes, she is.'

'Bundle is here as well, your dog.'

'Oh Bundle? Oh my God she survived too?'

'Yes she is well in the world of spirit.'

'Describe the dog' Charlie suggested.

'The dog?' she closed her eyes 'she is a Yorkie dog, with shining brown eyes, and a very shiny nose. She died of old age on the stairs.'

'Yes she did. We found her lying there in the morning.'

'She's a lovely dog. That is all I got.'

'That is very good!' said Charlie. Turning to Paul, Charlie asked 'Have you got anything?'

'I don't know if I have yet. I see a lady with a young girl.'
'That's fine. Can you describe them?', asked Charlie.
'I think I can.'
'Well do so', prompted Charlie.
'The lady is wearing a brown dress, and a lightweight, green shawl. She is wearing a hat, and she is 5' tall, with small feet, and small eyes. She died of pneumonia. The girl is about eight years old, and she is wearing a long dress, and no shoes. I see them together, hugging each other. She died in bed during the Blitz, and her name is Annie. The old lady is her grandmother.'

Charlie interrupted by asking 'who is the message for?'
'I don't know' replied Paul.
'Can anyone here understand this?' asked Charlie.
'Yes', a middle aged lady said, as she raised her hand. 'I do. She was my aunty, and my niece was Annie, and they died in the Blitz. The house was gutted by fire, but despite this they found the bodies.'

'You, next', said Charlie, pointing to Steve. 'Have you got something for me?'
'I have a message for you, sir.'
'Well, let's hear it.'
'Your grandfather is here, and he says he is George, and Mary Ann, she is claiming to be your mother.'
'Yes, I understand, please continue.'
'They are showing me a red brick building in the East End of London. It's a very old and cold tenement, and a place in Kilburn, again small and cold. A lady called Sylvia is here, wishing you well. She claims to be a friend of your mother.'
'Yes I understand, she was.'
'Who is Gladys?'
'She is a cousin, on my father's side. Thank you so much, Steve.'

'Now I give you a message' said Charlie, pointing to Lynn. 'I come to you young lady. You have just lost your mother. She died of an overdose. She says it was an accident, and that she didn't mean to do it. She forgot she had taken a dose before.'

Lynn wiped her eyes and replied 'Yes.'

Now Tim and David came through with information.

'Your twin brothers who died at birth, they have been named.'

'Yes, I understand that.'

'Who is Polka?'

'My terrier dog. I grew up with him.'

'I can see a child's buggy.'

'I lost a child.'

'Rosemary is here, holding out a rose to you. She is your sister.'

'Yes, in a few days time it would have been her birthday.'

'And a Geraldine is mentioned.'

'A friend here. Thank you so much.'

The energy is withdrawn.

'I come to you', pointing to a tall man, seated. Even seated he was tall. 'A Colin is here, and he says he loves you so much. He is your father. He went over very quickly, and he had no time to say good-bye.'

'Yes, that's true.'

'Evelyn is coming through. She died in a mountain accident.'

'Yes, it happened in the Scottish Glens.'

'She fell to her death. She says she was your best friend, and was more like a sister to you.'

'Yes, she was.'

'And Ricky is here, with Eva.'

'Oh, my God, my uncle and aunty!'

'Who was Mark?'

'My father.'

'And the name Wilson is coming through. That is his name.'

'Yes.'

'The name Armstrong is given, and he claims to be a friend of your family.'

'I understand.'

'I leave you with that.'

'I come to you', pointing to a young man in his thirties. 'Sir, Lucy is here.'

'Oh, my grandmother!'

'She is bringing Joseph with her.'

'Yes, she would.'

'He is your grandfather. He is giving me June 20th as an anniversary, and February as another one. He was born in 1899.'

'Yes, he was.'

'You were the only grandchild, and your mother was an only child.'

'Yes, that true.'

'Your father is mentioning the name Arthur.'

'Yes.'

'Who is Adam? He is on the earth plane.'

'A friend I work with.'

'And Kathy to the earth?'

'His wife.'

'The name Harry is also mentioned.'

'Yes, their small son.'

'You are a born healer, you will do well, and my guide is saying that you will do well!'

'Thank you!'

'I will leave you with that', and he turned towards a lady in her late forties. 'Ellen is here, and Rebecca has called out. Do you understand this?'

'I can take the Ellen. I think Rebecca was my great grandmother.'

'Good! Who is Mrs. Davey?'

'My next door neighbour.'

'There is a message for her, please pass it on to her. Her husband is here, and he is saying hello, and no goodbyes. Does the name Hobson mean something?'

'Yes it does. He is my boss in the factory where I work.'
'And Norman?'
'A friend.'
'Matthew is here now, and he died under very unusual circumstances.'
'Not really.'
'Yes, he says they were!'
'No.'
'Yes, he took his own life! He jumped off the 4th floor! Well now I will leave you with that, and all of their blessings are sent to you!'

It is now 1950, and a time of great changes. Charlie looked at his diary, and saw that it was full of bookings. 'Well it is nice to be so busy', thought Charlie. Charlie had given up his job at the Newspaper office, to spend more time teaching at the College of Psychic studies. The college was in a fairly imposing building in Kensington, No 16 Queensbury Place, and was run by Ivy Northgate.

Charlie ran day classes in the college, and some evening ones, in-between engagements. His engagements took him to churches all over the country. He had numerous engagements in and around the London churches – Eltham, Fulham, Lewisham, West Norwood, Wimbledon, and at The London Spiritual Mission. Outside London his engagements took him as far west as the Channel Islands, and he travelled northwards as far as Scotland. 'God will give me the strength to do my work!' thought Charlie.

He met Gordon Higginson, and Albert Best at The London Spiritual Mission. They had long debates regarding the state of spiritualism, and where spiritualism was going to. They discussed the Great Demonstration of Healing to be held at The Royal Albert Hall, with Harry Edwards.

'Good old Harry', said Gordon 'Do you know him?'
'Who doesn't', said Charlie.

'I know him too' said Albert. 'He comes to Scotland, and we have met on a couple of occasions in Glasgow. He's a lovely man.'

'Yes, he is', said Charlie.

'Good for him', replied Albert. 'Well, it is time for changes.'

'Yes, it is indeed', said Charlie and Gordon.

'We must look forward to better days ahead.'

'Yes, we must', said Gordon with a smile.

'I'm off to Wimbledon Church tomorrow', said Charlie. 'I'll bid you both a goodnight, and God be with you both!'

They parted at the gate, and Charlie hurried home. The night air was fresh, and the wind began to blow, and fine rain began to fall.

The following day Charlie arrived at Wimbledon Church, early as usual. He enjoyed his cup of tea, and relaxed as he chatted with Mrs. Baker, the Medium's secretary.

'Well now, tonight we have an open circle', she said.

'Yes, but I prefer the closed ones' said Charlie 'It is an experiment. Some people cannot sit regularly in a circle, so they come to an open one. They bring all kinds of influences with them, and not all are positive at all.'

'I agree' said Mrs. Baker.

'If you don't mind, Mrs. Baker, I need to be alone now to relax, and call my guides to my side.' Charlie closed his eyes, and started with an inner prayer, and kept his eyes shut. He heard people starting to arrive, and ignored the laughter and small talk about him.

Despite the noise getting louder, Charlie remained focused. As the people went into the church, they started to shuffle chairs around into position. On the wall surrounding them were all kinds of inspirational pictures, smiling down on them. The Seven Principles of Spiritualism were also on the wall, along with a picture of Jesus, a world teacher and Patriarch. A picture of Buddha, sitting in the Lotus position, also adorned the wall.

These pictures were all there for one reason only – spiritualism embraces all, and judges no-one. What a wonderful concept of life. If you feel it is right for you, then go for it. Spiritualism is a way of life in which to help others. A spiritualist never criticises any other orthodox religions – the choice is up to each individual. If only the other religions would do that – live and let live!

The evening was peaceful, and when Charlie walked through the door, the students were already seated. 'We will switch off the lights, but leave the red light on, Mrs. Baker, thank you', said Charlie. He sat down in a large chair, and addressed the students.

'Close your eyes please, all of you, it is important to attune all our energies together.Is there anyone present here who has never taken part in a circle?' asked Charlie. Silence followed.

'Then we are ready to begin' said Charlie 'we are asking for the protection of the white light around us, to seal us with gold and our spirit friends, guides and teachers from the other side, so we shall be inspired, and be happy. Contentment is the key word. Work together in peace and harmony. Let us harmonise by holding hands to create energy. Feel the energy coming from the person next to you, to your right, and to your left. When you feel energised, let go of their hands and place your hands on your lap, feet on the ground, back straight, and start to breath in slowly for a count of three, and breath out slowly at the count of three. Keep your eyes closed until you are impressed by spirit. Hold the thought, but if you feel you want to speak, be free to do so, by opening your eyes. Thank you!'

Some time had passed, and he kept watch over the meditating students, his eyes on the church clock in the semi-darkened room. Some of the students started to fidget a bit, and shuffled their feet, breathing heavily. He was looking around him, to see if someone was ready to speak, but said nothing.

A large lady, in her late forties, opened her eyes 'I have a lady here, and I am with a lady called Mary, in this circle.'

Mary hesitated to reply but opened her eyes 'Yes, I am Mary.'

'Phillip says he is here, and he is showing me a merry-go-round at a circus…..taking me to Ealing Park. He says he lived in West Ealing.'

'Yes, he did.'

'He is also saying that he didn't mean to do it, he just did it, and it was wrong.'

'Yes', Mary said 'he is my cousin, and I understand.'

'He is giving me the initials B.P.'

'Yes my mother is Barbara, and Paul is my brother living.'

'He talks about a child in spirit, a boy.'

'Yes', Mary said, 'he was stillborn.'

'His name was Zak.'

'Yes', said Mary.

'Phillip said he was named after your father.'

'Oh yes, exactly after my father.'

'And Eric is here, too.'

'Well now, I am not sure about that', said Mary 'I will check with my parents.'

'Eric is not a person, he is a parrot.'

Mary started to think 'Yes, my uncle had a parrot, but I am not sure what his name was.'

'They are fine, the parrot too. He was over a hundred, when he died of heart failure.'

'Thank you, and God bless you!'

Now Margo started to talk. She was quite an elderly lady, sixty at least. Her voice was growing manlier as she spoke 'My dear friends, I am White Eagle, greetings to you all.'

'Greetings' murmured the students.

'I come from the light to be with you all tonight. I come to let you know there is a wonderful world of joy that awaits you, beyond what you call higher life! In our spirit world there are many dimensions. In the lower astral plains life is similar to yours, but the further you grow spiritually, the lighter it gets. We have wonderful mountains and springs, gardens so full of beauty, and we also work. There are many of us that are assigned to help each of you, here. I have my own medium here, but sometimes I come to gatherings like this. I bring you love, and light, and progression to you all! I cannot stay long, but I am so happy to be here with you, sincere and very honest seekers. The world, your world, needs people like you, and the spirit world needs you too! We need you to connect, and give solace to those who are grieving, and are lost. Your world is full of darkness, and ours is full of light. You have to learn to love. We have already learnt that in that earthly school of yours, what you call life, aim high my friends! Be good to each other, and your rewards will be given to you in due course. Do not fret when life gets too difficult! It is all part of your earthly lessons here. It has to be the way it is. I must go now, and so I bid you all farewell. God hasten your earthly steps now. Goodbye, friends, and good night.'

Everyone in the hall remained very still after his departure.

1980

Just another number, and another year. Spring turned to summer, and the birds were singing in the back garden. Buzzing bees were busy gathering honey. The garden had become a tapestry of colours. The rose tree and the wild cherry tree were in blossom. The creeper was making its way nicely up the back fence. Charlie thought it would provide him with a bit of privacy. How nice God's world can be, especially in the summer time.

Charlie had turned eighty now, and time had really passed by very quickly. No time to look back, only forward. Always forward! He felt good and eager to teach more, and to see many tomorrows, yet to come. He never got married, and so had no wife, or children. 'Well, I suppose nobody will really miss me', Charlie thought. That is the way his life had been planned. In the past Charlie had had the opportunity to marry, but somehow it just never happened.

People often visit Charlie, more so now, as he had moved to a nice, large house in Willesden. It had a bathroom and toilet and three large bedrooms. He used one for his bedroom, but the other two rooms had a purpose. In one he kept his large spiritual library, and he also had a large desk, covered in glass, and the walls were covered with postcards that had been sent to him from all over the world. The other room, which was downstairs, was used as a healing room, and Charlie also used it for his sittings. He had plenty of leafy plants all over the house, as Charlie believed it was good to see nature inside. They also kept the house clean and healthy, providing oxygen.

He spent a great deal of time on the phone nowadays, with his mediumship readings. It was always good. Most people cried a little from relief and happiness, because they had been re-united with lost loved ones, however short the time.

Charlie was contented, if not happy. 'Well, I will be going home soon', he thought, 'and at last, I have achieved, here, what I was guided to do.' His mind was a collection of thoughts from the past, was it good, bad or otherwise. Some had happened slowly, others quickly. 'I have made some good friend here, and that is good. I have helped thousands, and that is even better. If I have missed out on something I do not feel it, so, therefore, I have not. I worked, and I did what I thought was personally important to me. I wonder what my Guides will say when I get there. Have I done well?' Charlie's thoughts were interrupted by the sound of the door bell.

'Mr. Charles?'

'Yes.'

'I have an appointment with you at 4p.m. I'm a little early, but do you mind if I come in?'

'Yes, please come in.'

'I am Marcia.'

'Yes, Marcia, please come this way.'

They went to the library. 'You can put your jacket over there', said Charlie, pointing to a nearby antique chair, solid, dark wood.

'Yes, thank you', replied Marcia.

'Please sit down here, opposite me.'

Marcia was about forty-five years old, and had lost some of her youthful figure. She looked very unhappy indeed. 'Happy people do not come to see me – they have no need for it', Charlie thought. 'Only the lonely, unhappy or very lost souls seek me out, but that is alright. Let it be.'

Charlie reached for his pint glass of water, closed his eyes, and he began to talk, 'Maude.'

'That is my mother.'

'Wait a minute; she says she owned a fish shop in Coventry.'

'Yes, she did.'

'She died of pneumonia.'

'Yes.'

'She died in the hospital. Nobody could help her, it was too late.'

'Yes it was', she said.

'Your uncle Charles is here as well. He is showing me a small monkey.'

'Yes, he did have one in Kenya.'

'But he came back to this country, where he died.'

'Yes he did.'

'He says he was cremated.'

'Yes. He was afraid of burials.'

'He is giving me an April and December anniversary.'

'Yes I understand' she bowed her head.

'And Alice is here too. A small lady, who is claiming to be your aunt. Is she?'

'Yes, she is.'

'She walked with a stick.'

'Yes.'

'She says she had cancer in the leg and knee. It had spread bit by bit, and she went quickly towards the end.'

'Yes, I remember that.'

'They love you, and bless you!'

'Thank you, Mr. Charles', said Marcia placing a £20 note on the table.

He never asked for payment, but one has to eat and pay the bills too. Somehow the money was always there when he needed it. He walked to the door with her, and said 'Bless you', and closed the door. He made his way to the kitchen to make a cup of tea. It always helped as a pick-me-up. He looked at the clock, and it was nearly six. He was expecting someone at six, so he went to sit down on the garden bench. It was shady by now, but balmy and calm, and very peaceful. He closed his eyes and prayed.... went up to the Spirit World in meditation reaching higher. He was asking what was the next person coming for, and praying that he could help him. Asking for his spirit loved ones to attend with him. John, that is his name. Charlie only asked for first names when any one called him. That way no one could accuse him of anything, not even a phone number. The less you knew about the person you were trying to help the better it was. That was the old school thought.

We can all agree on that – mediums young or old. People in the Spirit are well informed. You are going to see a medium, and they are arriving with you. Not all will know who is there, but the ones that are free, and ready to communicate, will. The less a person expects, the more they will receive from a sitting or session with any accredited medium.

Charlie looked at the sunset, which was fast disappearing now behind the ancient 45' high horse chestnut tree. Charlie thought that the tree needed cutting, but remembered it served as a house for many birds and two squirrels. Charlie decided to leave the tree alone, because where else would the wildlife go. He returned to his seat, and waited for Alex. The doorbell rang, and, as Charlie looked through the peep-hole, he could see a tall

young man standing by the door, and let him in.
'Take a seat', Charlie said.'
'Here?', asked the young man.
'Yes, over there', said Charlie.

Alex looked at the two large leather armchairs, and he also noticed a small round table, which had a vase in the middle, filled with some cornflowers, and some puffy grass. 'Was it pampas grass', Alex thought, 'well who knows', and he sat down.

Charlie closed his eyes. 'I see better this way', he explained. 'I see your mother is here. She is 5' 4" high, and has brown hair. She died of stomach cancer. She is giving me an August anniversary. Wait, she says it is the 7th ,and also a November one, the 18th of November. She says she is fine now, and she has met your father, and an anniversary is coming up.'

'Yes' said Alex. 'My birthday.'

'Sending love to Lorri.'

'Oh' said Alex 'Lorri is my horse.'

Charlie chuckled 'What a name for a horse!'

'Oh yes, but that horse can run and jump. He is a born show horse, and I love him.'

'There is Betty, saying hello!'

'Oh, that's my mother's name.'

'And Eddie is here, too.'

'My uncle Eddie. Thank you!'

'He says he died by falling in the bathroom, and hitting his head on the bathtub. He was found a week later, and his body was starting to decompose badly. Luckily I wasn't in it, he says. He still has his lively sense of humour! He says he slipped, and he was not drunk, as he never drank any alcohol of any sort.'

'Well as far as we know he did not', said Alex.

'Another lady has just come. She is wearing an organza dress, and has a large cameo brooch in her lapel.'

'My grandmother.'

'Her name is Anna.'

'Yes, from my mother's side.'

'A very lovely lady. Her hair is in a bun, and she has lost a lot of hair, because of her illness.'

'Yes, she had cancer.'

'She has lost a lot of facial and bodily weight, too.'

'Yes she had. I went to see her in hospital.'

'Lung cancer.'

'Yes, she smoked.'

'She is sorry now she did it, but she says she is fine, and would not come back here, for all the tea in China. She sends you her love!'

Alex thanked him, and left £15 on the table. Charlie turned back from the door, picked up the money, and put it into a shoe box that he kept especially for that purpose. He carefully placed the shoe box back inside the wardrobe, and shut the door. He made his way to the kitchen and made some tea. Lovely! His chest started to feel very heavy. 'Oh, my lungs', it was hard to breathe, to take a full breath now. 'I better get to bed', Charlie talked to himself. He pulled the cover over him, and fell asleep. He was woken up by the sound of the phone ringing.

'Mr. Charles?'

'Yes' he answered sleepily, and looked at the clock, only 7.30 a.m. 'Oh no, it is not my time for conversation over the phone' he thought. 'Yes it is, Charles. Who is this?' he asked.

A frantic voice on the other end of the line revealed all. 'I have to see you, please, today.'

Charles said 'O.K. do come. I will see you at 1 p.m. Does that suit you?'

'Yes' said the voice on the other end of the line.

Mrs. Cotton arrived at ten minutes to one. 'Oh, she is in a hurry, but I suppose it is better to be ten minutes early than ten minutes late' thought Charlie.

'Come in, Mrs. Cotton.'

Both sat down in the comfortable chairs facing each other.

'Give me a minute, Mrs. Cotton', and Charlie shut his eyes. 'Your husband is here, Malcolm. He says he went just a few weeks ago. He believed in the other side. He is a well read man, and talks about law and order.'

'Yes, he was a lawyer.'

'That figures' said Charlie. 'He was a lovely man, kind and considerate, but he liked his own way. April, he is giving me an April anniversary, and February. He talks about "little heaven". He loved the place, and he liked fishing there, whenever he could find the time, but he had always thrown the fish he caught back.'

'Yes he did. Thank you!'

'He is wearing glasses. Who is Mrs. Gerard? He is talking about her.'

'Yes, she is a friend.'

'Your friend needs you now, he is saying go and see her, she is not well.'

'I will.'

'He talks about Australia, Brisbane, and he sends his love to Paul there.'

'Oh god, my nephew.'

'And love to you from all of them!'

The session ended abruptly, with nothing to add. 'Well, if they don't want to talk any more, that is that', Charlie thought.

Nicholas knocked on the door. 'Mr. Charles?'

'Yes, what do you want?'

'My mother sends you some cake.'

'Thank you son, that is very nice of her. Thank you!' He was grateful. He was getting very old, and very tired. He had to sit down more often now. 'The old legs can't carry me as well as they once used to. Look at my white hair, how very fast time has flown, by heaven, very fast.' Not all his days were happy ones, but when he gave survival evidence that was good! Next door's poodle barked a few times. 'Bill…oh Billy. Pity, I never managed to own a dog, but I have done other things. And now at eighty it is too late to get one, as he would probably outlive me. That is the way of the world. That is life here. We grow old and weary… a little shaky, but not shaken… have to slow down.' He pushed that thought from his mind, as he needed to teach more to enable him to pass on his experiences to others. 'Oh, yes', he thought. 'I will have to write a book… my memoirs, or a book on the knowledge that I have gained.'

He got up and made it to the bedroom, and put his head heavily on the pillows, turned on his side, and slept. There was a frequently recurring dream he'd had for the past few months. He saw his mother coming towards him. He saw the tunnel and he went through that ever- knowing light. It felt so good and warm and cosy. He did not want to come back. The aches and pains left his body… he floated… and embraced the light. He saw his father coming towards him. 'Welcome son', he said, and he knew he had arrived. He was home. He looked around him just as he thought he could see, some wonderful warm sun-like sun lit up the whole place, but it was not the sun shining over the earth plane. It seemed a different dimension, and a very different sun shining. Same unknown source, giving heat and light, which felt every so comforting, and welcoming at the same time.

'We go through here', a voice said, but Charlie could not make it out who said that. It seemed like a crystal maze, glittering, but it was all so warm. A beautiful blue bird flew towards him, and settled on his shoulder. The bird started to talk to him .'You are home now, and I am yours to keep.'

A huge brown dog appeared 'I am yours too, Charlie, to keep', said the big Newfoundland dog. 'You always wanted one like me. My name is Theo.'

Charlie bent down, and patted Theo's neck.

'We are going to your home', Theo said. 'I live there, too.' They walked through sunny, golden fields, heavy with the scent of flowers, and the bees were humming, flies were flying, and butterflies spreading their heavenly wings. They stopped outside a beautiful bungalow. There were roses everywhere. 'Rose Cottage' wild roses running up all the way to the windows.

His mother took his arm. 'Come now, Charlie, this is your home now.' George stood by the door.

'Father' Charlie said, 'at long last we meet again!'

Charlotte, looking young, came running to the door. 'My dear Charlie, we have missed you so much, but, you see, it has all begun here, and it all ends here. Come now, you have worked hard for that. You have earned what you see now. In your past earthly life you have helped so many, dear boy! You can meet all your friends tomorrow, old and new. Your guides will show you around more tomorrow, and you can begin your new life, here, with us.'

'Welcome to the Spirit World, my boy, which you have served so well, and now let the magic begin in the life which is everlasting, with that spiritual sun, which never goes down. Enjoy the offerings; you have earned it, my son. Here all is love and light. You worked for that all your life on earth, now enjoy the benefits.'

Charlie looked around, and asked 'What about if I wanted to be a guide for someone like I used to have?' Charlie got what he asked for. A guide came close that seemed very familiar to him.

'There is your medium, Charlie', he said showing him a photograph, which seemed to be alive. A young boy, aged ten. 'You will watch him grow, guide him and help him all his life. If that is alright with you?'

Charlie replied 'I would not have it any other way!'

EPILOGUE

This story is written from the heart. Soul to soul, spirit to spirit.

Agnes Freeman is a well known author of spiritual publications. Her books: *They Walk Beside Me*, *The Fledglings Way to Mediumship*, and now *Charlie*.

She is also a journalist, and a spiritual medium. She has helped many people worldwide. She has worked in the U.S.A., Canada, Australia, Hungary and Great Britain, and she also resides in Great Britain.

Whenever there is a cry, she tries to wipe away your tears. When there is human suffering, she tries to alleviate it. When there is an animal suffering, she can help as she is a healer, animal healer, and also a pet psychologist.

Love and Light

Printed in the United States
19460LVS00001B/176